The Thin End of the Wedge

Bonnie Forester

08 . 10 . 2019

With love to my
Godmother Carole
x

The Thin End of the Wedge

A Mother's Experience of Anorexia

BONNIE FORESTER

THE CHOIR PRESS

First published in the United Kingdom in 2019 by
The Choir Press

ISBN 978-1-78963-064-0

Contents

Contents

Acknowledgements

I would like to thank my husband and my daughter Emily for their support and encouragement in helping me to write this book, my daughter Shelley for being courageous enough to help me share this book with others, and various family members and friends who have read the rough draft and encouraged me to publish. I promise that everything you read is true and meant to help fellow sufferers.

To my two wonderful daughters

Introduction

There is a well-known saying, 'Be careful what you wish for!' I can verify that this is very true. In 1976 I was doing my degree course and teaching certificate, with the main subjects of English, maths and education. I clearly remember one wintry morning sitting with my English group and tasked with writing a short story. I stared at the paper, mind devoid of ideas, while those around worked furiously, brimming with inspiration. In the end I wrote a tale about a girl called Ellie who only existed in my imagination. I knew it was bad, but my thoughts were only confirmed when I heard the offerings of my fellow students read out loud; one had written about the trauma of an appendectomy, another about the harrowing loss of their father, and they were all so very good, so convincing and built on passion and personal experience. I remember thinking that nothing memorable had ever happened to me and sent a silent prayer heavenward that I could have some similar experiences to inspire me to write from the heart, with truth and integrity, so that I might produce something worthy to be read.

Now, many years later, my request haunts me and I wish I didn't have the catalogue of terrible life events that could move me to write with raw emotion: death of parents, death of an unborn baby, divorce etc. Worst of all was the near-death of my firstborn daughter, Shelley, aged eighteen, from anorexia. It was a time of living hell for both of us, a wilderness devoid of all hope, as I faced my crippling inability to do anything to save her. Or could I?

Finally, I was moved to write the events down as a personal catharsis, a warning to others and a support tool for those facing the same trauma with a loved one. I write with the hope that, if just one person is helped through reading my story, it will have been worth it.

It has taken a few years since I wrote this to gain the courage to get my book published, and it is with my daughter's permission that I now share her terrible experience. It is awful to read so much news about mental health problems in the world, and especially among the young and vulnerable who feel they have nowhere to turn. We must open our eyes to those who need support, listen to them, push aside our own prejudices to listen to their innermost torture and offer the hand of help and friendship. Sometimes it takes tough love, but inaction is not acceptable; the sufferer must always be the priority.

Finally, please read the afterword, for there is a happy ending where life is apparent and hope reigns.

Thank you.

PART I

Leading Up to the Illness

CHAPTER I

Shock and Realisation

October 12th, 2001, my forty-ninth birthday. A day of planned celebrations and hopefully a joyous family occasion – but, sadly, nothing could have turned out to be further from the truth. Instead, my 'present' was the beginning of a nightmare scenario which would almost destroy my daughter, our family, and all the visions and dreams a parent can have for their offspring. It was the day when part of myself died too, resulting in a life that could never really be the same again for any of us.

The day started normally enough: tea and toast in bed, brought as always on such special occasions by my wonderful, loving second husband. Cards were opened, presents exchanged and, despite the inevitable middle-aged doldrums about being 'another year older' and the fear of the 'big fifty looming', I was looking forward to our planned shopping trip and meal.

After my divorce in 1989 and subsequent remarriage two years later, my twin daughters, who were now aged eighteen, saw their natural father whenever he was close to our area, as he lived and worked away. It happened that one of his scheduled visits, seeing friends in a nearby city, coincided with my birthday. This posed a slight dilemma as the girls wanted to see him but also wanted to join in my birthday celebrations. An easy solution had been decided upon which was acceptable to all parties. We would all travel to Hepford, the girls, who could now drive, in their car, and my husband, my parents and I in another – my elder daughter Shelley (the elder by seven minutes!) taking a couple of passengers to ease the load. On reaching Hepford we would leave the girls to spend time on their own with their father, meeting up again later to go for the meal. Everything was arranged, and I was planning to enjoy spending all my birthday money on some retail therapy!

I was just making some finishing touches to my make-up when Shelley went to post a letter, and as she passed the window on her way to the box my stomach lurched sickeningly. I was shocked to the very core. She wore black trousers and a red top and looked stick-thin. The image that registered most was the thinness of her legs and her inability to keep her trousers up, so that her pants were almost entirely showing. In that one shocking moment it all made sense, realisation hit – *my* beautiful daughter had an eating problem. I hadn't concluded that it was anorexia, but something had happened – overnight, it seemed – without us being aware. It was like an alien invasion of her body which had suddenly sucked out her very being, reducing her to someone I no longer recognised. I couldn't believe how she looked.

When she returned from the post we questioned her state of health and expressed our grave concerns, to be greeted with open hostility and a refusal to discuss the situation. I asked her to at least change into some more appropriate clothing before she met her father, as I knew he would be as mortified as us to see such a change, but to no avail. I suggested a compromise such as her wearing a belt or maybe pinning the waist, but she was defiant; no changes would be made. I reasoned that her father might be shocked and embarrassed to see her pants showing, but her response was dismissive – she would go as she was.

I wondered if she was making a planned statement, demonstrating attention-seeking behaviour towards her father, but now, in the light of experience and better information, I think it was more likely to be flaunting of her new 'slim self', a warped notion of looking good which many anorexics possess – even when others look on in dread at their emaciation and frailty.

I can almost sense your derision, reader, even hear you cry with disbelief, 'How can a mother watch her daughter, who lives with her every day, become thin and ill without intervening, without even noticing?' I agree, you are justified in chastising! Your reaction had been my own reaction every time I had picked up a magazine or seen a television programme featuring the story of an anorexic: *What are the parents thinking of? Why have they allowed things to get this bad without getting help?* But, until you have personally experienced the insidious nature of the eating disorder and the way it penetrates highly intelligent minds like some malignant force, allowing a person to so skilfully deceive their loved ones and themselves, you cannot begin to judge others.

Of course there had been concerns and we had offered

advice, but we had been in some parallel universe which seemed to keep us just far enough away not to see the full horror of what was happening.

It had begun simply enough. Shelley had got her first job in a city office and wanted to fit in with her 'executive counterparts'. She had consciously tried to lose a small amount of weight gained during her rather sedentary two years at college. She had also joined a gym to tone up her shape. We had encouraged the move, knowing it would help to bolster her rather low self-esteem and raise her confidence. To this day, though, I don't understand how this positive move transformed her from a beautiful, perfect, intelligent young woman, with the whole world at her fingertips, into this waif who was challenging me and refusing to cooperate, even in the face of my very real horror.

CHAPTER II

A Most Precious Gift

My beautiful twin daughters had always been every-thing to me, a gift from God.

I had married at twenty-three and in 1981, five years later, gave birth to a stillborn son, seven months into the pregnancy. I was distraught, crying and working myself silly to ease the pain, compounded by the fact that less than a week after the funeral we had to move away with my (first) husband's job, to Hertfordshire. It was a diffi-cult time, but my neighbours were amazing and I was quickly reminded of the old saying that 'there is always someone worse off than you'. I met people who had lost both a husband and a child, or several babies, and gradu-ally I stopped feeling sorry for myself and got on with my life again, even getting a new job as a proofreader with a publishing company ten miles away. The longing for another child was ever-present, though, and when I found that I was to work alongside someone who was a few months pregnant, I thought life was just too cruel. However, Moira and I became firm friends. The joy and tribulations of her pregnancy became a shared experi-ence, and Fridays the day we went to the local pub for a jacket potato and soft drink!

I remember one frosty morning, five months after the

stillbirth, having an argument with my husband. He stormed off to work, and I returned to the bathroom, where I sobbed and screamed for some time. I honestly thought I had snapped, gone insane, and made my way to the doctor's, sure he would suggest some drastic action. He was actually very reassuring, considering I had told him I thought I was mad! He said that at last my shock and sadness over losing my son had revealed itself and that now I would be fine, able to rebuild my life and look to the future. I was given vitamins to boost my nerves and he suggested that as there were no signs of future pregnancy, I should record my daily temperatures, so that any possible ovulation problems could be identified. I had something positive to focus on again; I would have a baby!

My peace of mind was short-lived because two weeks later my husband was told he had been made redundant, approximately six months after we had left behind a home we loved to 'move with the job'. It had taken us eighteen months to sell our house, numerous trips to view properties with me in the throes of morning sickness, and eventually leaving our baby son's grave many miles away, now to find it had all been for nothing – no one is indispensable. We found ourselves living in an expensive area with no family ties, no money and no direction. This was compounded by the death of my husband's mother, his final parent, a week earlier, something else which we were struggling to come to terms with. We had seen her in a coma, had been told it could be weeks before anything happened, and had returned home, only to find the next day she had died. I remember being overcome with grief at the funeral, both for her and, if I am honest, for my other loss. Everything was crowding in, divisions were blurring, and we were both on emotional overload. I remember my husband walking away, crying desperately, and yet pushing me away to grieve alone. Perhaps that was an early indication of our future break-up, but if it was I never saw it then.

It certainly had been a bad few months. Arguments got worse, no baby was imminent, and at last, greatly demoralised and chastened, we decided to move back in with my parents until a new job could be secured.

After about a month, my husband got a job in a 'new town' about fifty miles away and off we went again with renewed hope. I consulted a doctor before we left about the temperature charts I had been keeping for six months, and he said it looked as though I might need fertility treatment. He advised me to seek out a new doctor as soon as possible and pursue it when I had moved in.

On my thirtieth birthday – am I sensing a pattern here? – I duly consulted my new doctor, showed him my charts and endured lots of embarrassing questions, such as whether my husband drove a lot or wore tight underpants! It was agreed that I would be referred to a gynaecologist and I would receive an appointment shortly.

Imagine my astonishment and delight when less than a week later I discovered I was pregnant and, with great irony, needed to change the gynaecologist's appointment to one with the obstetrician! Many theories were explored as to how, after all the months of waiting, I was finally pregnant (and, before you say it, I don't mean the obvious!). Was it 'new house syndrome'? Perhaps, as some of the locals believed, it was the tubs of prawns that were served up on a Saturday night at the local pub, which certainly seemed one explanation for the explosion in pregnancies in our particular area!

I didn't care; I was on cloud nine. Nothing could make me happier. But something did. In the fifth month of my pregnancy I went for a routine scan and was given the amazing news that I was to have twins. I was so excited I even forgot to visit the loo after drinking a couple of pints of water! I had to get home; I had to tell the world!

CHAPTER III

Were There Any Signs?

Shelley and Emily were born in June 1983, Shelley at 18.06 weighing 4lbs 12oz (sorry, I still can't think in metric weights!) and her identical sister seven minutes later, weighing 6lbs 13oz. Apart from the two of them being breech births and narrowly escaping Caesarean section, all went well. When Shelley was born they placed her across my chest and I remember experiencing exquisite joy and huge relief, not to mention surprise, as I had been convinced I was carrying twin boys! I remember how alert she was for one so small and how she focused her eyes on the world around her, a fact that even the delivery staff commented on. Then she was whisked away to intensive care while I prepared for her sister's hasty arrival.

I was reunited with my daughters at around 23.30 in the intensive care suite. Shelley wore a little knitted pink bonnet and looked so tiny. I was handed two whimpering bundles to hold, one under each arm, and remember the tears streaming down my cheeks. Looking back, I ruined all the first photos of my new arrivals by looking a total wreck!

As they grew up, the girls were just like any others. Hard work, full of mischief, but worth every moment.

Their father left us when they were only two years old, their granddad died of cancer when they were three and a half, and then their father returned. We remarried, believing things would work out, but by the time they were six we were back to a family of three again. Yes, it was a terrible time emotionally and I did find it difficult to cope, but I had to keep going for my daughters. They needed love and stability and as settled an existence as I could give, and I was determined to give it.

I managed to get a full-time job as a mathematics teacher in a local school, and that proved to be our lifeline. Everyone there was kind and helpful and sympathetic to our situation, and gradually we could rebuild our lives.

It was tough being a full-time professional and mother, but financial stability, a home and a car made all the difference. I always tried to put the girls first, ensuring that I was home as soon as possible at night, any gaps being filled by the parent of a friend of theirs from their school. They had all the support I could give and their parents' evenings, reading slots, sports days etc. always took priority.

Their childhood seemed to be progressing normally with just one full-time parent, their father taking them out every other weekend. School reports were always excellent and the girls were happy. I remember one birthday when money was tight and their 'party' was a few friends, a paddling pool and boiled eggs with soldiers! I still have the photos of their happy, smiling faces in their stripy Mickey Mouse swimsuits.

When the girls were eight years old I married my current husband. Emily and Shelley were bridesmaids, reading during the church service, resplendent in their respective pink and turquoise dresses, which took on a hint of profiterole by the end of the reception! They immediately took to Glen; he taught them to ride bikes, took them swimming, and drove them to and from ballet, gymnastics and music lessons. He had a sixteen-year-old daughter and a twelve-year-old son who lived with his ex-wife, but they both welcomed the girls and shared their dad.

Our honeymoon consisted of one night in the honeymoon suite of a hotel in the Cotswolds, followed by picking up my girls and Glen's son Rick and going to a flat in Bournemouth. We played cricket on the sands and in the evening went to the Festival of Lights in the park; everyone queues for a taper, then lights as many of the tea lights as they can find attached to frames around the park. The finished result was a fantastic, magical display of boats, swans, flags, flowers etc. flickering in the darkness, amidst a sea of excited faces all pleased with their efforts. It was here that Shelley, Emily and Rick were bought fluorescent necklaces, perhaps invented by some panicked parent who at some stage had lost a child or two in the melee – more likely yet another scheme to fleece unsuspecting tourists and their pestering offspring. The three glow-in-the-dark children returned to the flat and proceeded to 'do a play', which consisted of them donning pyjamas and glowing necklaces and bouncing on the pull- down bed, while we applauded loudly. These were happy times, family times, normal times.

And so life went on for several years in a continuous round of careers, school life, holidays at home and abroad, birthdays, barbecues and *normality*. During this time the girls still had free contact with their father, although he moved around a lot with his profession and didn't always see them on a regular basis. Sometimes months would pass without any word, but this didn't overtly seem to bother them. He also had a few relationships, and his partners were kind to Emily and Shelley. The two of them seemed happy to go on outings and short breaks.

Both the girls did exceptionally well in SATs and GCSE exams and seemed well set up for the successful future I hoped would bring them security. They remained impenetrably close as only twins can be but became more individual as well.

Shelley was arty and loved to reproduce Salvador Dali's painting *Metamorphosis of Narcissus*. Looking back, it seems almost prophetic that she should be so taken with the subject of self-obsession, something she was later to encounter as a destructive force within her own life. She was also a very accomplished pianist and achieved grade five, but she was always modest about her talent and, although a good performer in local concerts, was clearly not a natural exhibitionist. She enjoyed a long spell with a local silver band, playing the tenor horn, and seemed socially quite comfortable throughout this period.

Shelley had become less conventional than her sister in

her dress and hair and loved to exact comment for being a bit zany or different. Sometimes this aspect of her character caused arguments. She was an enigma, very private and shying away from notice at some times, and yet strangely 'in your face' at others. She was almost two people, one of whom we understood but the other a manifestation of her intelligence and artiness and, more sinister, an inner struggle which we then didn't understand and could do nothing to halt.

Emily was always quite conventional in her behaviour and dress. She too was musical and a very accomplished clarinet player, but early on she decided she did not want to progress through her grades or give performances. When she was sixteen she fell in love. I don't know whether this last point was contributory or not, but Emily decided against university, adamant that she would get an administrative apprenticeship and train while earning some money. She did exactly that, leaving school and going straight into employment with a local authority, gaining good qualifications, confidence and the respect of colleagues on the way. She seemed to grow up, become self-assured and have purpose in her life.

Looking back, this may have been a more difficult time for Shelley than we imagined. She and Emily had always been inseparable, always within easy contact, but now her sister was working, had money and was spending most of her free time with her boyfriend, leaving Shelley feeling isolated and less mature. We thought she too might decide to get a job and enjoy academic freedom. However, she adhered steadfastly to her dream of going to university and obtaining a degree in environmental science. She maintained her Saturday job in a local supermarket and was looking forward to her A-level course at a local college.

There were few outward signs at this stage that she was troubled; a few arguments, yes, because she manifested spells of awkwardness and became difficult at times. Routine doctor's checks culminated in the conclusion that we were experiencing the 'terrible teenage years' and that medically nothing was amiss. We continued to weather the storms of happy parenting and hoped that college would bring calm seas.

CHAPTER IV

Turbulent Waters

College seemed to be the answer to all our prayers; Shelley was at long last taking the A-levels she needed to fulfil her dream of going to university, and we would get space from each other and the difficult times that we had recently been experiencing. Shelley signed up for geography, psychology, biology and general studies, the biology choice being somewhat of a surprise as she had shown most talent in the arts and humanities areas at school. She was aiming for a degree in environmental science and felt her choices gave a spread of disciplines.

She seemed happy enough as she went off for the bus with friends, sporting baggy jeans, sloppy jumpers and zany hairstyles, but this 'happy' picture would eventually became far from that. Her clothing would become her ultimate uniform as an anorexic, bagginess concealing her true body shape and giving a false sense of wellbeing.

Days and weeks passed and we seemed to settle into some kind of normality. Shelley's work was of a high standard and reports were good. She continued with her part-time job in a local supermarket, and by her birthday in June she was able to get started on driving lessons: yet another layer of independence. During this time, however, it felt like there was no real bond between us. It was like an invisible screen which allowed us to see all that was going on but was sufficient to prevent the contact and closeness that a loving relationship should have. This was foreign to us because we had always been a loving family that shared everything and had no secrets. Now we were being shut out by some kind of polite veneer.

It was like experiencing the calm before a storm, with the storm a few miles off yet, feeling we were safe and comfortable and yet knowing that soon, without warning, something would happen. But, as we were told, you expect such behaviour from teenagers! So we tiptoed on some kind of knife-edge, quite glad when our paths kept us apart and surviving in an atmosphere of relative peace by avoidance of confrontation.

It became obvious throughout this first year how much of a perfectionist Shelley was. She was very uncomfortable and unhappy if she got anything less than an A grade on any piece of work. Her tutor regularly told her that she did not need to aim so high, as indeed did I, for as an ex-teacher I have seen the consequences for pupils who try to push themselves too hard, but our entreaties fell on deaf ears. All this hard work culminated in Shelley winning the prize for most promising first-year student in the college, a prize sponsored by one of the local companies each year. We were, of course, the proudest parents in the world, but did not at that time realise how much this honour would eventually cost.

We had survived the first year at college and I was hopeful that we could spend some 'quality time' together during the summer holidays, but Shelley had other ideas and at the time I would have been wrong to judge her for having a hidden agenda. She announced that she wanted to get her second-year coursework completed over the holidays. As she was doing geography she had to decide on some kind of comparative study analysing how something impinged on local tourism. She had decided to focus on the impact of cycle tracks in the forest area where we lived and needed to carry out comprehensive surveys at different locations in order to obtain relevant data. I embraced this to begin with, thinking that she was keen and focused and I at least could help her achieve her aim, but I didn't realise that she would want to be dropped in lonely locations for most days over a series of weeks. I made sure she took food and drink and a mobile so she could ring when she was ready for collection. I was worried about her being vulnerable and always made sure she sited herself near to a road or house. I know the surveys were carried out and a myriad of questionnaires completed, but I now wonder whether she also needed to isolate herself, fill up her time so she was in control of all she did. Of course, once the data was collected, the report and subsequent analysis had to be written, and so the isolation continued in her room.

We did manage a week's holiday in Bournemouth with Shelley, Emily, my parents and my husband's mother. The day before we went was extremely significant, although I didn't realise it at the time. We had gone to a retail park to do some shopping, and Shelley and her sister were walking ahead of us. My mother made a comment that

Shelley had put on a bit of weight or looked a little plump in what she was wearing, assuming she was out of earshot, but apparently the comment was crushing and consolidated her warped self-image and low self-esteem.

It was probably after Shelley's illness, when her sister confided in me, that I learned how devastated she had been by the comment and how unaware we had been. A simple remark, however lightly meant, can often cause devastation in the onset of anorexia. To this day my mother is mortified that she ever uttered such a tactless comment and has often said she will forever feel guilty, but I know now that such triggers are many and varied. They would usually be quite trivial to the unwitting perpetrator or to a well person, but to the anorexic they are another chink in their already crumbling armour.

The holiday itself proved to be good, with Shelley eating well, joking about and seeming to be her 'normal' self, but the time bomb was already ticking and about to explode.

CHAPTER V

Shattered Dreams

During the summer holidays my stepson, Rick, asked if he could move in with us for a few weeks as his mother had to move house and he didn't want to leave his friends in the village. We readily agreed and he made it quite clear that he was happy to occupy any room and didn't want to disrupt our current set-up. Everyone was pleased to have him with us, and after some discussion it was decided that Shelley would move her bedroom downstairs. She had been requesting a change of room for some time and also had her piano, so we thought this would work out well. We also assumed she would be going to university in a few months and so arrangements would be different anyway.

Obviously we wanted to make it her personal space, and we needed to order some wardrobes and drawer units as all the bedrooms upstairs were fitted. We asked her to accompany us on the shopping trip to order the necessary items, but she had no interest in coming, instead telling us roughly what she wanted. There seemed to be no motivation, no interaction. I duly ordered new quilt covers, and very soon the room had her identity and was a comfortable space for her.

The time came for Shelley's return to college in the

autumn term, for her second and final year, and I believed that the completed coursework would give her confidence and a head start. Sadly, the reverse was true. She returned home on the second day and seemed a broken person. Apparently, and contrary to what Shelley had told us, the coursework didn't need to be completed for some time yet. The upshot was that her tutor had all the time in the world to comb through the work of her 'star pupil', resulting in many modifications being listed for Shelley to make. In her wisdom the tutor was aiming for the highest possible grade for Shelley, but in my daughter's already troubled mind being told that all was not 'perfect' was disastrous. Instead of focusing on the positive – a good piece of research, volumes of data and a rough draft to follow – she saw lost holidays, negative reviews, failing standards and loss of face. She was distraught, inconsolable, and, worse, she refused to see things rationally or to talk the problems through; instead she became withdrawn and spent long periods alone. Eventually, I did manage to find out that all was not lost and that the tutor had made her aware of what needed to be done to make the study right.

Over the next week Shelley laboured tirelessly to create perfection, even at the expense of everyone around her. I remember Rick's twenty-first birthday, when all the family had assembled to see him open his cards and presents; all except Shelley, who insisted on working on the computer, in the same room, and was quite dismissive of the happy occasion going on. At the time I was angry, because you only celebrate a birthday like that once, don't you? Years later I feel such compassion for Shelley and for all the hurt and isolation she was feeling, but hindsight is a wonderful thing!

Shelley eventually produced a study that contributed to an A grade at A-level, but to her the work was 'rubbish'; it was a sullied creation and something she no longer felt proud of. In the world of the perfectionist, second-best, even transformed to best, is never quite the same; it will always be the product of inferior workmanship.

After this, things went from bad to worse. Shelley spent more time in her room, opted to eat her meals separately and generally cut herself off. Even her sister found herself increasingly shut out of her confidence. Arguments became increasingly hostile and often we came close to physical blows as communications broke down and her moods became more unpredictable. Her lights would be burning at all hours of the night as she strived for perfect standards in her college work. Many nights I would go downstairs at 1am, having seen a light on, and find her working, only to see her still there on a visit to the loo two hours later. So arguments spiralled and relationships became more strained. Around this time she had started dating her future husband Neil, and at this stage she became more defiant towards us and more reliant on him.

Towards Christmas things came to a head. With exams looming, every waking moment was spent on revision. Gradually every wall was covered with pieces of old wallpaper covered in copious revision notes, in the miniscule writing which had now become Shelley's trademark and seemed to be symbolic of her shrinking self-esteem. She wouldn't take a break and was clearly getting exhausted but just couldn't seem to stop. More arguments ensued.

Then one evening the balloon went up; she wanted to give up. She no longer wanted to take her A-levels, go to university or fulfil any of her longed-for dreams. She was angry, tearful, confused, and we didn't know what to do. She wanted to leave home, she said, and she thought she would move in with one of her school friends, an option clearly not open to her.

I too was at breaking point after months of worry over her. In a fit of temper I told her to go; I even got the suit-cases for her and told her to start packing, saying her only option was to go to live with her father in Middlesex, a suggestion she vehemently fought against. I couldn't stand any more. For months I had worried, not slept, taken abuse, been rebuffed, been told by her sister that I was not giving her enough attention, and now she wanted to walk away and leave an earthquake zone.

I ran out into the woodland at the back of our house. It was pouring with rain but I didn't care; it was cleansing and purifying and preferable to the choking feeling I found indoors. My husband came after me and I told him I didn't want him, to leave me alone.

When I returned half an hour later I was calmer and felt more able to cope and talk things through, realising now that Shelley was crying for help and needed us after a long period of denial. I was chilled to the bone, and met a tearful husband who thought I no longer wanted him either; he hadn't understood my cry for help and my need for solitude. We talked things through, reassured Shelley that we didn't want her to leave home, and agreed she should leave college if that was her true decision. And so it was decided. We wondered if this decision had anything to do with having a boyfriend, wanting money and freedom perhaps, like her sister, but we never shared such thoughts.

The next day I took an unprecedented step and contacted her tutor at college, to fill her in on current events, express our concerns and prepare her for Shelley's visit. The tutor said she had been about to contact us because the previous day Shelley had been close to tears and not her usual buoyant self. We both agreed she had been working too hard and didn't need the consistently high grades she had been intent on getting. The tutor suggested advising Shelley to take her exams so she would at least get certificates for all her hard work, albeit AS-levels. This was discussed and the exams were taken with a view to Shelley leaving ASAP, but, for whatever reason, once the exams were over she decided to stay on at college to take her A-levels and giving up was never mentioned again.

CHAPTER VI

A Change of Direction

After Christmas life seemed to settle again. Outbursts were fewer and we all gave each other a little more space. On a positive note we discussed applications for university, but Shelley showed little urgency in this direction, even though she said it was still what she wanted to do. She did say she now wanted to go to university nearer home, perhaps travelling on a daily basis to lectures, and since she was soon to be driving we thought, somewhat selfishly, that this was a better option for her. We assumed her long-lasting relationship with Neil and her close bond with her sister were contributory factors in her decision. So it was agreed that she would apply nearer home and prospectuses were sent for.

One day during the Easter holidays we made an appointment to visit her favourite choice, but when we got there she showed little enthusiasm for the place, the curriculum or the staff who were trying their best to inspire her with what the university had to offer. It was hard work for her, them and us.

Shortly after this she began to get confused and difficult, and we were again the 'villains of the piece'. A typical episode was when she told her father on a visit that we were 'in her face' and that we made too many decisions for her. You may reach that conclusion yourself, but in reality we were only acting on information Shelley had given us and were just playing the dutiful parents by trying to help meet her requests.

If I describe one incident you may begin to understand our dilemma. Shelley had told her father that she did not want us to pick her up from her supermarket job on Thursday and Saturday nights unless she asked us to, bearing in mind that she worked three miles away and did not yet drive. We agreed to this on Wednesday night. Thursday evening came and reached eight o'clock, Shelley's expected time home. She did not turn up. It was dark now and after another half-hour we began to worry. We assumed Neil had picked her up and decided to go to the supermarket to make sure she was not still there, checking lay-bys on the way for Neil's car. We just wanted to know she was safe and would have driven by as long as we knew where she was. There was no sign of her at work or along the way, and concern began to mount as we live in a village area off the beaten track.

A further half-hour passed and I was beside myself when I suddenly heard a car pull up outside. It was a taxi with Shelley getting out. Relief! At the same time the phone rang and it was her father, checking to see how the new regime of 'backing off' was going. Shelley came into the kitchen in a rage and grabbed the phone. Close to tears, she told her father we had left her waiting in the dark and hadn't turned up for her, that there were no buses and that she could have been raped or something for all we cared. I was flabbergasted and so was he, and he reminded her that we had done precisely what she had asked us to do. I think that was the first moment that he realised that we were not as black as Shelley had painted us and that she had some real issues.

As with all things the episode blew over and life went on. Shelley was booked for a driving test but was devastated when she went for a pre-test lesson and could not get back to the test centre due to extraordinary roadworks that caused chaos that day. As we learned afterwards, they had resulted in most tests being cancelled and rearranged. She was given an early retest date but still talked about 'failing her test' even though she hadn't actually taken it! Matters were made worse when she then went on to fail the actual test, especially since her sister had passed first time. She delayed applying for her retest as exams were looming at college, and seemed to turn against the idea of driving, another of her so-called failures in life.

The exam period came and Shelley went to ground, shutting herself away for long periods, to be expected when sitting four A-levels. She had also started to go to the gym and we actually thought at the time that this might help with the stress, so we encouraged it. We didn't see much of each other but she seemed to be coping well.

A new bombshell at this time was that she no longer wanted to go to university but wanted to get a job instead. This was what her equally bright sister had done and she seemed to be doing well, so we went along with her decision. After her exams Shelley went for an interview with a large building society group for an administrative role, and after all the battles we thought this was probably a wise decision and encouraged it. In reality it would be one of the biggest contributors to her illness and she would almost die striving for the perfect corporate image.

June was the month of the girls' eighteenth birthdays and a time when my and Shelley's relationship had almost been restored. I decorated the house with balloons and we organised a family meal complete with special cake. The girls enjoyed it very much but were overjoyed to be old enough to go clubbing for the first time with their older boyfriends. I still have the happy photograph of both girls holding '18' balloons and dressed to party!

Shelley looked really good and healthy. She had a short red skirt and a black shiny top with open slashes in it and had such a perfect figure, as did her sister, that she was every mother's nightmare manifestation of the teenage temptress! But we knew the boyfriends well and knew they would keep them safe.

I felt a great sense of relief that I had got my 'little girls' to adulthood safely, something I had vowed to do when left on my own with them, but I felt desolate too, knowing that they were lost to me now. From now on they would be free to make their own mistakes and successes, but always there to make me proud.

Shortly after this, Shelley and Neil went on a short break together, prior to her starting her job, and looking back on the holiday snaps she looked relaxed, happy, slimmer but perfect. She had suddenly become a stunning beauty, very photogenic and very much a young woman.

When she eventually started her new job she looked smart and every inch the executive, and I had hopes that this was to be a happier phase in her life. Unfortunately, the new job proved a new pressure. She felt inferior to many of her new colleagues and began to diet and exercise more to try to attain some perfect image. At the time we only saw the slight weight loss and had no conception of the inner workings of her mind. A further failed driving test did nothing to raise her self-esteem and only sent her for yet another punishing session at the gym, not even coming home to tell us how she had got on. She was a self-perceived failure and no amount of reassurance from us would change that.

August was a better month. I was proud when Shelley asked me to go to get her A-level results from college and thrilled to be the first to know that she had four magnificent passes. A week or so later she passed her driving test at last and we helped her get her first car and the independence she so desired. This too proved to be a tool in almost destroying her life, but at this stage we were still ignorant of this.

Around this time, Shelley became secretive and isolated again, her car giving her freedom to go from work to the gym without us being too aware of how her time was being spent or of her gruelling exercise schedule. You may say that we must have noticed changes to her body, but anorexics are clever at concealing their figure beneath sloppy 'casual wear' and she had also begun to enter a phase of wanting her privacy. She said her hours of work prevented her from eating with the rest of us and she preferred not to have reheated food, so she would get her own. This, of course, took away my control over what, and if, she was eating.

And so, reader, we reach the place we began, at the point where I realised my daughter had become ill without our being fully aware. If you recall, it was not the forty-ninth birthday present I had expected. It would begin the nightmare phase where we came to grips with anorexia and its ruinous nature, the thin end of the wedge that drives families apart, destroys hopes and dreams and, more terrifyingly, can damage the sufferer's reasoning skills, self-perception and grip on life so that they can no longer control what is happening to them. If you dare, get on the ride of death and grip the bar tightly, because you will not be prepared for some of the horrors that faced us from that day onwards.

Thankfully *this* ride will not end in death and hope-fully reading about the experiences which follow may in some small way raise your awareness of such issues, help you to understand those things which we took so long to recognise and accept, and make you more tolerant and proactive in helping any individual you may find who is suffering a similar fate to Shelley. If lack of ignorance makes you effective in saving just one life, then Shelley's life has been far from a failure. So *please* read my account of her story with compassion, for I know now, in these late days, that my compassion was not enough; not until now, that is.

CHAPTER VII

Aboard the Rollercoaster

The Sunday following my birthday was a difficult time for us all. We needed to discuss what had happened and how Shelley had become so ill so fast, but we didn't really know where to start. Obviously, concern was expressed and the idea of some plan of action broached, but it was no easy task when Shelley did not acknowledge that there was a problem.

At first Shelley was hostile to the idea of needing help, and then she became tearful, vulnerable and childlike, needing to be cuddled and receptive of affection. In this less hostile state she said she realised that she had lost some weight but didn't feel ill; in fact she felt good about herself, but said she would try to eat more healthily from now on. She said she was probably a bit tired and run down but nothing more.

And so we left it and everyone returned to 'normality' on Monday morning. However, for us it would be a time of watching and monitoring, as alarm bells had begun to sound.

The new week showed little improvement, Shelley continuing with her many visits to the gym and still eating 'secretly'. When the weekend arrived I thought I would try a new approach. Perhaps Shelley had been right; she had worked hard, she had achieved at the highest level, and perhaps she did need a rest. Being in a new job meant that holidays were difficult to arrange, but I thought I would venture the idea of a short break.

When Neil arrived on the Friday evening I suggested they do something spur-of-the-moment like a weekend away – *now*! The idea met with some resistance at first but gradually began to form in their minds. I said it would only take a few minutes to pack some essentials and that I would foot the bill. That seemed to swing it; clothes were hastily packed, and they were off to Neil's to pick up his spare underpants too! They promised to telephone later that night to let us know they had arrived safely and where their destination was, working that out on the way!

Later that night, they telephoned from Torquay; they had found a comfortable hotel with a blazing log fire, important to Shelley since intense feelings of cold had been an issue for her in recent weeks. Neil told me that she had eaten a plain jacket potato, her now staple diet, which was reassuring, but we were slightly disconcerted to hear that they had walked for a couple of hours, visiting the harbour etc. It seemed she could not drop the exercise regimen. Still, optimistically, I hoped they would both return refreshed, restored and perhaps having discussed Shelley's problems and, with Christmas looming, begun to form some plan to improve her current lifestyle.

Shelley seemed happy on their return but within days had returned to her gruelling regimen of working and going straight to the gym. Her eating was not improving. She was becoming more skeletal by the day, and of course any talk of getting medical advice was treated with open hostility. I tried myself to see what could be done, but the answer was 'nothing'. Being over eighteen, Shelley had rights and I did not; basically, if she chose to get help it was available to her, but otherwise we could only stand and watch our daughter wasting away.

Sleeping became difficult for me and I spent many hours researching anorexia. I read about the symptoms; yes, they were all there, and then some! There were success stories, but nowhere was the chapter on how to persuade the anorexic to reach out for the help they so desperately need.

Life became difficult for us all. Shelley would not respond to our pleas and Neil seemed powerless to change her mindset, even though he too was suffering and wanted the old Shelley back. I never understood how Shelley could cook Neil a heaped-up plate of food when he came up for the evening, how he could eat it and she could watch him; I never wanted to eat when she was around! I now understand that anorexics 'feed' off looking at food, watching others eat, cookery programmes etc.

Because the changes in Shelley were so alarming I had insisted that she eat when we were around, so that in some misguided way we were reassured that she was at least eating something. That exercise in itself was a night-mare. She would sit in the sitting room with her back to a boiling radiator, eating her jacket potato, sometimes with beans. The gas fire would need to be full on as well, and even then she was cold. Often we would be almost passing out from the extreme temperature, but it would have been a brave person to venture to turn the setting down! I never understood why she wouldn't put on extra clothing instead, but for some reason this would not be tolerated. She would cut her food into tiny pieces and proceed to move them around her plate, resulting in about an hour and a half of her fork scraping over her plate, until our teeth were on edge. I wanted to shake her, completely the wrong response, but instead chose to leave the room before I could explode.

Another worrying development was the pacing – a kind of 'caged animal' activity. We don't know whether she was aware she was doing it, but it was yet another form of burning the calories.

This whole process became a way of life for Shelley and the more I tried to help, the worse she became. In fact she enjoyed causing an argument because then she could isolate herself and abuse her body, away from our interference. Relationships became tense between me and her, and between me and my husband. Even her sister Emily started to rebel because she felt Shelley was getting all the attention and no one had any time for her. It was true; our every waking moment was obsessed with what was happening to Shelley. Is anorexia an attention-seeking illness? I certainly believe it is an unconscious cry for help.

Finally, in December, I contacted the gym and tried to get them to stop Shelley attending. At the time they were most unhelpful and I got the line about her rights as an adult again. I pleaded with them to get her records out and check on her frequency at the gym, which had now escalated to two hours per day, six days per week, and asked them to look at how much weight she had lost – in fact, just to *look* at her. I got nowhere and with Christmas approaching was almost at my wits' end.

You can imagine my relief when, in early January, the gym telephoned me and said that they intended to ban Shelley from all the gyms in the catchment area until her health improved. Why the change of mind? Apparently, a local doctor had seen her on some equipment and had insisted she should be stopped immediately. He accomplished what I could not and I will be eternally grateful to him for being a step in the process of saving Shelley. Amazingly, it took me five long years to find out his identity and to thank him with all my heart.

Returning to Christmas, it was the events prior to, and during, this 'joyous season' which led to some decisive action and most certainly saved Shelley's life.

CHAPTER VIII

The Storm Breaks

To say that we were not looking forward to Christmas was an understatement. We were worn out from constant arguments, worry and lack of sleep, and this was compounded with my fear of what would happen on Christmas Day when the wider family assembled. What comments would emerge about Shelley's weight, what misguided and tactless remarks would be made, and how would I fight to keep the peace and survive the 'joyous season'? Being a Christian and a child at heart, I had always found Christmas a wonderful family time, but this year I dreaded it.

Christmas Eve set the scene. Because the gym was closed, Shelley did a long run instead and came back cold and exhausted. She had said she would eat Christmas dinner with the family (as she was vegetarian, that meant a lot less than the rest of us), and would therefore eat very little on Christmas Eve to compensate. Although not ideal, the situation was accepted; we had grown grateful for any small mercies.

Christmas dinner itself was a trial. Tables were resplendent with napkins, candles, holly etc. and Shelley got to sit separately with her sister as requested, but it was difficult for everyone. You didn't know where to look, what to talk about, and none of us enjoyed our meal. To make matters worse, it was obvious that Shelley was struggling to eat, eating to please us but not herself, and the process was taking forever. I wanted us to stay seated until she had finished, to avoid drawing attention to her, but the lengthy process was too much for the older members. In the end everyone was excused, with Shelley vowing she would finish her meal. She had been given a miniscule portion and the meal had to be reheated six times because it was going cold before she could manage it. In the end we called a halt and told her she had done very well, even though in reality she had eaten very little.

In the sitting room we began to open presents, but people were nearly passing out from the extreme heat. We weren't even allowed to have a door open. Eventually it was all too much and we had to have some air, resulting in Shelley storming off because her demands were not being met. Unfortunately, at that time we did not realise how desperately cold and miserable life was for her, and in any case she had opted to be like this, hadn't she?

Shortly afterwards the situation eased slightly for us. Shelley got a call from Neil to say that his granddad had been taken into hospital, due to a heart condition, and his mother had to go with him. In a flash, Shelley offered to go down to Neil's house and cook the Christmas turkey, as no one there had eaten yet. It seemed that she too wanted to escape from the situation. Apparently, she cooked a meal fit for a king, enjoyed by all – except her, of course – and all the washing up, tidying etc. was done single-handedly by her. There are many ingenious ways of burning calories! She returned much later, tired but calmer, and the rest of the evening was enjoyable.

Boxing Day was traditionally when we went to my mother's for lunch and tea, and this year was no different. Shelley said she would come to tea, and I knew she had eaten nothing until then that day. She arrived bubbly and ready to help with the preparation, whisking the cream for the trifle, cutting sandwiches. She was like a whirlwind moving around, offering out the delicious feast but taking nothing herself. The longer the charade went on, the sicker I felt.

After tea, with little heart, we set about the traditional party games: consequences, Scrabble etc. Traditionally, this was the time for passing around the nuts, chocolates, oranges and so on. Again Shelley was in her element as she weaved around, foisting calories on everyone except herself.

Finally, as she looked up at me with her skeletal jaws munching chewing gum, her only vice, I snapped; I couldn't bear it any longer. I told her the pain of seeing her was too much, I couldn't stand it any longer and I wanted her to do something, get some help. Instead of agreeing with me, she flew at me and said I had a problem. I was distraught, at breaking point after so many months, tearful and needing to get away. My mother thought I was wrong for 'having a go', for causing a scene, for upsetting Shelley, but I had had enough!

Glen said he would take me home and I didn't resist.

Being home was a blessing; I didn't need to gaze at the face of my dying daughter, and I didn't need to explain my actions. We clung to each other and I cried yet more tears – I was surprised they kept coming – and then we had a dilemma to resolve. We were due to go to London for a couple of nights with some friends the next day, travelling by coach, and I said I couldn't go; I had no heart to face it. Glen, on the other hand, thought it was just what I needed, especially after the drama of the day. He felt I wanted some space and that together we needed to discuss where to go from here. Reluctantly, I saw the sense of his argument and threw a few things into a case. The break proved to be what I needed and it was good to have time away from our normal surroundings to clear our thinking. We decided that the new year had to be the time when we became more proactive. We needed to fight the red tape and find a way to save our daughter. I returned home refreshed, hopeful and determined.

It seemed Shelley had done some thinking too and we returned home to more open hostility, silence and secrecy. Phone calls from strangers began and it didn't take long for us to work out that she was looking for a place to move out to. Although we had our suspicions we waited for her to tell us, but days passed and nothing was said until one Friday. She said she was moving out and into a room in a house just around the corner from Neil. I knew she was running away from the inevitable and so refused to give her my blessing, even though my heart was breaking.

On the Saturday, Glen helped Neil to pack Shelley's possessions into his car, a process which took several trips, but I refused to be involved. It was very unlike me, but I was so angry, hurt and devastated that helping would have felt like hypocrisy. I would not play happy. Instead I went out until after she was gone. I knew Glen would do all the necessary and give the support I could not give at that moment. It was probably the second hardest thing I have ever done; the first was yet to come.

Shelley had left me a letter trying to explain that she needed independence and that the last thing she wanted to do was to hurt any of us. Later that evening she phoned me and apologised and said that the move was something she needed to do. I knew it was the action of someone whose life was ebbing away, someone who was being destroyed by some evil force pervading her body, someone who was trying (consciously or unconsciously) to remove the possibility of being stopped on her journey to the inevitable. No matter what, though, I knew I would defeat this evil; I was not about to sit back and let my daughter die. When the phone call came it was a tearful reunion, a pouring out of love both ways, and even as I write this now I cry at the memory of how I felt at losing Shelley, at not knowing, daily, how she was. I consoled myself with the thought that she was only ten miles away, near Neil, and tried to fool myself into thinking that things might improve if she had some space.

Things didn't improve. I saw Shelley next at my mother's seventieth birthday party in January. It was a three-course affair for about thirty family members and should have been a happy occasion. It was held at a local pub and Shelley had said she would come at the end of the meal. I spent a stressful time trying to get around to all the people who had not seen her for some time, both to prepare them for the shock and to ask them to avoid making any comments that might upset her. She turned up looking smart, pretty and happy but heart-rendingly thin. She seemed to be wearing a public mask of wellbeing, but her form and pallor belied this. She was sociable and did her duty but did not stay too long. Her interactions with others were fine, except in the case of one person who took Shelley to one side and kindly gave her some money for a treat, but also expressed concern about me and my anxiety for her. It was well-meaning, but of course Shelley saw it as quite the opposite.

Later, as we drove back in Neil's car, it became very dark and foggy, and all at once, as is customary where we live, a deer jumped out in front of the car. Neil slowed and the deer crossed safely, but we weren't prepared for the second deer to follow. Unfortunately, we clipped her slightly and she ran off. Neil stopped the car, but she seemed to have gone and there were no signs of her being injured. We checked as well as we could, and once again I glimpsed the real Shelley, the caring girl with a heart of gold and a real concern for all of God's creatures.

Less than a week later, Shelley called by one evening with some news. This became the start of some real changes and the end of our worst nightmare. She was on the move again!

CHAPTER IX

Time Running Out

When Shelley had news, these days, it was usually about some *fait accompli*; decisions were all her own and there was no room for manoeuvring. At least this time she had told us her plans and shown us details of where she was going. The flat looked nice on paper and it was in the City, where she worked: a definite bonus point in my eyes, as it meant she would no longer be travelling fifty miles per day to her job. Lately, mysterious knocks and scrapes had started to appear on her small, vulnerable old car, and her explanations for them – never her fault, of course – were never too convincing. I was worried to death about the risks she was taking driving with a body so emaciated and a mind so consumed.

This time we encouraged the move and helped all we could. First of all her bed etc. had to be moved the thirty miles or so to the new flat. Shelley had gone on ahead and we arranged to meet her at the flat later. We loaded the hired van and were appalled to see the tiny room she had been calling home for the last month. The house was fine and clean, but there must have been no privacy for Shelley in her condition and with her social difficulties at the time. The owner showed a certain relief, I believe, at losing his tenant so soon and expressed his concerns about her severe health issues.

Along with the relief about the reduced travelling Shelley would be doing came the deep-rooted concern that she would now be twenty miles away from the family home if anything should happen, and seeing her now it appeared imminent. I just had to cling to the hope that her new flat would offer the independence and interest she needed to recover, and hopefully Neil would be able to stay with her there.

The flat was '*bijou*' but very nice and uplifting with its big windows. Shelley met us having toured the shops for hours, getting a sofa and all the comforts needed to create a home. Her taste was good and she had thought of everything, even a wall poster which warned of the destruction of planet Earth by greed; Shelley had always been concerned about the environment. We stayed a few hours putting the bed up, hanging the curtains, assembling shelves etc. The landlord called at one point and seemed refreshingly nice and mindful that Shelley had all she needed. After a space of time, probably when tiredness had set in, we began to get 'bitten off' and were reminded that she would finish off in her way.

We left her to her own devices, keeping in touch by phone, and just before the weekend she invited me and her nans to see her flat now it was in some order. We met on the Saturday and I was appalled to see a further deterioration in her appearance but of course could say nothing. The nans loved the flat and furnishings, and the afternoon passed happily enough. At one point we went to a superstore to get a few bits and I could see everyone staring at Shelley, appalled at her thinness; I fear some even thought she was on drugs or something. I am ashamed now to say that I was not comfortable being with her at this stage and felt as though I was being judged too. On the way home from her flat, of course, the inevitable comments came and the inevitable question was returned: what can I do?

After a terrible weekend I rang Shelley's office and asked to speak to someone in confidence. They said they were aware she had a problem, but as she was never late for work, performed at an excellent level and had never had a day off sick they could do nothing about referring her to occupational health. To this day I dispute this, but the last thing I wanted was to be blamed for her losing her job, although later she said her work had been a factor in her illness. I explained that she had recently moved further away and asked if they would at least let me know if she did not come into work and had not telephoned in or pre-arranged time off. She was so ill now that I was worried that she would collapse and not be found quickly enough. They readily agreed and, foolishly, I had a sense of temporary relief.

The next week was critical. We consulted various authorities about what to look for in the final stages of anorexia and reluctantly found out what we needed to do to section Shelley; it was the only thing likely to save her now.

The following weekend we arranged for her dad to pay her another visit and for her sister to stay for the weekend and try, as her closest, to persuade her to voluntarily seek the help she so desperately needed. Glen and I took a much-needed break away to plan what we would do in the event of the weekend 'summit' failing and decided that the following week we would arrange the section. Sadly, on the Sunday night when we met up, Emily said her attempts had been totally dismissed and we knew the moment we had been dreading was about to materialise. In a way I was glad; we would at last have the power to put a stop to Shelley's suffering, the power to save her life.

Armed with all the facts, we decided to carry out the section on the Friday. We visited her again on the Thursday to give her a last chance to go with us voluntarily to the hospital. We obviously could not mention our plans for the section or she would have flown the coop, a fatal act given her fragility; time was seriously running out.

When we arrived, unannounced, at seven in the evening it was like entering the world of the elderly. All the curtains were drawn, the lights were dim, the fire was full on as well as the heating and Shelley was huddled like a granny in her nightclothes in front of the TV. It broke our hearts to see her and I know Glen had to turn away and shed a tear, so much did it rip at our very souls. She said she had eaten, jacket potato and beans, but nowhere were the telltale signs of cooking aroma or washing up. When she was in the toilet, a place she frequently had to visit now, I checked the bin for leftovers – none – and the fridge – empty except for one satsuma and a bottle of water. Sadly, we had become as devious as her; we had to be. We were now convinced more than ever that the time had come to take matters into our own hands.

Glen made one final attempt. He put his arms around Shelley and asked her to go with us then and there to get some help with her problem. Her answer: 'What problem?' We hugged her, kissed her and left, taking away her broken hair dryer to mend, knowing that in a few more hours, God willing, we would see her again, only this time we would be in control.

CHAPTER X

What No One Should Ever Have to Do

On Friday morning I went to work; it was a training session on mathematics for learning support workers at a local school, and at least I was occupied to a point as I kept pace with the group work. Once home again (I only worked part-time now and even that was a struggle on bad days), I showered and we lunched, knowing that we were going to need all the strength we could muster to face the task in hand.

We had already decided that we would contact the out-of-hours team so that Shelley would be spared the indignity of being 'taken away' from work. The team had to consist of a medical doctor, who would consider her physical wellbeing, a psychiatrist, who would assess her mental state, and a social worker, who would be there to defend Shelley's rights: farcically, as far as I was concerned, even if these rights include killing herself.

What followed next was like a military manoeuvre. We drove twenty miles and parked in a car park used on market days, which we had decided would give us the privacy to make that all-important call. When I rang on my mobile and reached the social worker, I was treated almost with hostility and quizzed on why we had not called the day team out. I explained that we did not want to cause a scene at Shelley's workplace and was almost ridiculed, being told that she couldn't be as bad as we said if she was still working! To say the least, they were reluctant to take me seriously or to agree to come. Finally, after much pleading, the social worker 'graciously' agreed to get the psychiatrist to call me to discuss things, but finished by saying that parents are often overanxious and things are not as dire as they think.

I was devastated and bewildered. It had taken courage, weeks of soul-searching and immense planning to even get to this stage, and now we were being dismissed by the very people who were supposed to help us. I was almost in a state of shock.

We decided to drive to Shelley's flat whilst we awaited the call back, because I suddenly visualised the team agreeing to turn up and her not being there! Of course secrecy was the thing, so we parked around the back of the flats in a side road. Sure enough the lights were on; she was in. I then realised that her door, the only available exit, was around the back, and we had no way of seeing it from our current vantage point. So we moved, this time parking in a side road opposite the entrance door.

After what seemed aeons, the psychiatrist rang back. I explained everything again and said that Shelley was about five and a half stone and desperate. The psychiatrist was pleasant and understanding but still felt, in view of Shelley still working, that her situation was not as dire as we feared. In the end I told her that she was my last hope, that if she didn't agree I knew Shelley would die and that I would pay her call-out fee if necessary. I told her one look would be all she needed to be convinced our actions were right. Eventually she agreed but said they would be about half an hour because they had to locate the missing link, a medical doctor.

We waited for what seemed a lifetime, and then I reminded Glen that we were a long way from the road and if Shelley decided to go out with Neil – it was Friday night, after all – they would be gone in the car before we could get to them. So we decided to mount a vigil behind a bush on the street corner! If it hadn't been so serious it would have been funny! A man passed us with his dog and we said, 'Good evening.' Ten minutes later he returned and we were still skulking about like some ageing Starsky and Hutch. We invented a story about waiting for someone to return to the flats and he went home satisfied, hopefully not to report us to the neighbourhood watch!

A few minutes later and the worst possible scenario struck: Shelley and Neil emerged in their Friday night glad rags and made for their car. Then it was all a matter of quick thinking. We rushed forward with some muttered gabble about returning the repaired hairdryer and me needing the loo – anything to buy us some much-needed time. Shelley wasn't happy – they were off to a local quiz night – but reluctantly let us in.

It was then the hell began! We needed to stall them until the team arrived without alerting them, because flight would most certainly have ensued. Shelley is an intelligent girl and I am sure she soon realised what was going on. We went over old ground about her illness, talking about anything just to buy us more time. She was getting angry and I knew we were up against it. I sent Glen a sign, asking him to check whether the lights had been turned off on the car; he sensibly picked up on this and used his few minutes away to check on the progress of the team. Apparently they were five minutes away.

Things started to get ugly; Shelley knew. She was frantically trying to get Neil to take her out. Eventually I had to bar the door and face the consequences of her fury. She told Neil they were over if he didn't get her out. I believe at this stage he too knew something was happening but knew, like us, that if he was right it needed to happen for Shelley's sake.

Finally, after what seemed like eternity, the doorbell rang and the wait was over. The team of three walked into the room and Shelley shot me a murderous look, but I didn't care. I had done my job; now it was over to the experts. They all seemed shocked to see her and I became more positive she would get the help she needed.

The doctor examined her and seemed satisfied, asking her to pack a few things. With that Shelley seemed to go quiet, resigned almost, and got on with the job. I offered help and was repulsed; so was Neil, and we had a hard job convincing Shelley that he hadn't known of our plans. She wasn't being very nice to him; he had let her down, and when I tried to comfort him, his shaking frame racked with sobs, he bodily thrust me away. It looked like I was no one's phone-a-friend tonight!

It had been vital that Neil didn't know of our plans; he

loved Shelley so much that in his misguided way he would have warned her and helped her escape, even though his judgement advised him otherwise. Anorexics are powerful, persuasive people. Emily had known, of course, and had to be trusted to keep the hateful secret. Like us, she knew it was all that could save her sister and was prepared to suffer any backlash to this end.

There seemed now to be a war of minds between the team; they seemed to stare at Shelley, at us and each other, saying nothing until eventually I had to ask what was happening. I was told that she would be sectioned, a consent form was signed, but it was evident that the social worker couldn't wait to use his power of veto on Shelley, all set, as was his remit, to defend Shelley's right to freedom, even though her mind was disturbed.

We waited for a further hour for the ambulance which we needed to take Shelley the mile to hospital; because of the threat of cardiac arrest she was not allowed to make the journey by car. When the ambulance team arrived they escorted her away gently and in jocular manner but were given short shrift for their trouble; Shelley went in silence, talking to no one, accompanied by Neil.

We followed in our car and as we turned into the final road I reacted with alarm; the buildings all had barred grilles over the windows and looked like some grim leftover from a Dickens novel. I suddenly lost nerve, feeling I couldn't do this to Shelley, but realising it was out of my hands now. A few yards further on and I realised to my relief that the psychiatric hospital had been rebuilt and a welcoming, modern building was waiting to receive Shelley.

We were ushered into a waiting room and told to wait. We took the opportunity to let Emily and her father know that Shelley was safe. It was now ten o'clock and the proceedings had taken a total of five hours!

After a quarter of an hour, someone came and said that Shelley did not have to see us if she didn't want to and that we would be given no information about her case unless she agreed: more rights. Also, we were told that Shelley could immediately appeal against the section, but that they would oppose her decision if it would be detrimental to her health. Were they on our side? I was confused, but I thought so.

Eventually, Shelley did want to see us and looked happy in rather a nice room. She said she had expected barred windows and feeding tubes but was reassured now that there were none of these. Then, as though our nerves were not already in tatters, Shelley announced that she and Neil had become engaged, *there*, *now*, a result of a heart-to-heart at a very sensitive moment. We hoped it was genuine and not a knee-jerk reaction, but were only pleased for now, pleased she was safe, hopeful they would have a future. And so began the hospital stay which was to last four months, up to Shelley's nineteenth birthday.

Half an hour later we were in a local pub; Neil and I had jointly suggested we really needed a drink, and brandy was the only thing to quell my shattered nerves. Neil said he was glad that we had done it, Shelley was so ill, but like us he had no real stomach for what we had just witnessed. We were all entering a period of separation from Shelley, hopefully a positive time, but somehow none of us felt like celebrating.

PART II

Treatment Begins

CHAPTER XI

Things Can Only Get Better – Can't They?

Surprisingly, I slept well that night, through both utter exhaustion and sheer relief; now we were to get some-where, now Shelley would get well again.

The feeling of security was short-lived. At around eleven o'clock Shelley rang in a panicky voice. A doctor had been to see her and they had finally weighed her; she was 4st 6lbs, at a height of 5'6"! I found the news hard to take – we had never believed she was this low, and slowly the horror began to sink in. Again came the waves of guilt, of self-blame. How could I have allowed my 'little girl' to become so ill? Surely I could have done more?

Shelley also said they had tried to take a blood sample, but her veins had become so small and fragile in response to her abuse of her body that they could not get blood in the conventional way. Instead they had inserted a fine capillary tube into her groin, and that had resulted in a massive swelling, but still they couldn't obtain enough blood for a kidney-function test. They would try again.

She said she needed to eat fruit as soon as possible and asked me to get some. I was off like a shot to the local shop for oranges and grapes. This was the first time my daughter had asked for food in about six months. I also picked up some magazines and the prettiest flowers I could find. We were on the twenty-mile journey to the hospital as soon as possible.

We found Shelley, suitably chastened, in her private room overlooking a pretty garden. She was calm but obviously shocked by her blood-taking experience and her weight. However, in spite of the urgent call to get her fruit, none of it was touched. Apparently they had now succeeded in getting a blood sample. She had an enormous swelling in her tiny leg and was about to get a most magnificent bruise.

She was bright and took us on a tour of the accommodation block for the mentally challenged. There was a very pleasant day room with a TV and lots of books, games and puzzles. There was also a second smaller one, where review meetings were often held, and a large kitchen/dining area where most 'guests', apart from those receiving sedation, were allowed to roam freely and make snacks for themselves or visitors. The whole place was very cheering, considering the preconceptions we had; it even had a table-tennis area!

Shelley said she had to meet with the head psychiatrist, who would assess her mental state and decide on the length of her section order. Later we marvelled to see her eat a small portion of beans on toast and to do it with ease. I could feel myself becoming ten years younger; she would be OK.

I asked Shelley if she would like me to help her with a bath and washing her hair when I came the next day,

Sunday, and she was keen on the idea and asked me to sort out some nice shampoos. We parted as a family should, lots of hugs and kisses, and the mood was upbeat.

On our return the next day, Shelley was cuddling with her dad, who had finally arrived. She seemed more her old self and had made a few friends; it was good to see her socialising again. She had been weighed and bloods taken and it appeared that, miraculously, the abuse to her body had not been as destructive to her organs as we had feared. There did seem to be some kidney weakness and she needed to pass water many times per hour, and this pattern was to continue for a few years.

Leaving the rest of the family to their own devices, we set off for the arranged bath. I don't think I could ever have been prepared for what I saw. When Shelley undressed I was shocked to my very being. She was literally just bones with skin stretched over them. Gone was her beautiful bust; in its place now was a young boy's chest, flat and sunken. However, it was her lower regions which shocked the most. In her pants she looked like an Ethiopian famine suffer and the fabric hung like some token loincloth. The incongruity of seeing a women sporting an 'eleven-year-old's body', but with pubic hair, was even more shocking.

I ran the bath, but she was too weak to get in and had to be helped, and it breaks my heart even now to write about the pain she was in. She couldn't even bear the hardness of the bath against her poor bones and we had to make a nest of towels in the bath to cushion her. She was like a Dresden figurine and I was almost fearful of touching her in case she broke. However, we carried on, washing her hair, and by the end of the procedure she was pleased but totally exhausted. For my part I had one of the closest experiences of my whole life with my daughter, but also an indelible image that I will carry to my grave.

Again we parted in upbeat mood; it had been a good weekend, and Emily had shared some long-overdue closeness with her sister too.

When we arrived on the Monday afternoon there was a chill in the air. Shelley was sitting in the smaller day room and seemed tense and troubled. She told us that the psychiatrist was happy that she had no really worrying problem other than the eating disorder, and was transferring her to the general hospital, on the same site, for a re-feeding programme, under the guidance of a dietician and eating disorder expert. She was not happy and sat with her bag packed, focused inward again. We assumed we could transfer her the few hundred yards across to the hospital by wheelchair but were told she needed an ambulance, as they still feared cardiac arrest.

I did have one light moment when Shelley was off on one of her loo breaks. One of her new acquaintances, a manic depressive who had been in and out of hospital, commented on what a lovely girl she was. 'She's a pretty girl,' he said, 'and a lovely person, but she could do with eating a bit more!' Bless him, I don't think he realised that was why she was there.

After a long wait the ambulance drivers arrived and popped Shelley in a wheelchair. Just as before she wouldn't speak, ignored their enquiries and made the journey in sullen silence, although this time I was in the ambulance with her. I felt embarrassed, but I suppose they had seen it many times before.

When we got into the hospital the ambulance crew parked the wheelchair near the shop and asked us to wait while they booked her in. To my dismay, when they were gone Shelley promptly got out of the chair, wearing a cellular blanket, and said she was going into the shop for 'a look around'. I was horrified and frightened but no amount of entreaty would get her back. People were staring; did she like such attention? When the crew returned they too were shocked to see her gone, but, as I said, they were probably used to it. I wasn't and I could see we were in for a bumpy ride again.

Shelley was booked into a side room opposite the nurses' station, so they could keep an eye on her. She was told she would be started on liquid food supplements and would be weighed daily, and she was also going to be offered counselling. Once she knew she would not be force-fed and that she had some control she relaxed again. The room was in a tower block but did have a view and a TV.

Once Shelley was settled the staff nurse sent for us. It was then we received the bombshell. Shelley's section order had been lifted; she was free to go if she chose, but they hoped she wouldn't. I was livid, scared. We had gone through all this for what? We had to hope that she wanted to live, that she wanted to get better. If she didn't we were once again powerless.

It was made clear to Shelley that she was in real danger of cardiac arrest at her low weight, and for the moment she seemed prepared to stay the course. However, she was becoming hostile towards us again and the nurse told me this was common. She said there were a lot of similarities in anorexics: they tended to be highly intelligent, artistic and highly abusive to their mothers. She told me, if I turned up to visit and Shelley did not treat me well, to go home again. She said it would be a long trial and that I would probably bear the brunt of it, so survival had to be my main aim too. She turned out to be so right. There certainly was a lot more hardship to come!

CHAPTER XII

Beginning the Long Haul

I managed to get the Monday off work and we began to sort out various elements of Shelley's life, left in the wake of her illness. We began at the letting agency. Obviously her stay in hospital would be a long one and she agreed that she needed to give up her flat. She had only been there two weeks, and had paid a month in advance and a further month as a bond; it was not going to be easy.

As it happened, for once in my life, I was rewarded with the milk of human kindness. The agency proved to be extremely sympathetic, had noted she did not seem well, and could see the strain we were under. Of course a contract is binding, but they said they would do their best to find a replacement tenant within the month. We arranged a meeting with them on the Wednesday to do a handover inspection.

Around lunchtime of the same day we went to see her employers at the building society; Shelley was adamant that she would not return there and wanted to give her one month's notice. I have to admit I felt more than a little angry towards these people; I thought they could have intervened and suggested that Shelley get some help much sooner.

After a long wait, we were ushered into a windowless room with a member of the personnel department. She said they were obviously aware of Shelley's problem but had seen no reason to act on several counts. Her work was impeccable; she was always punctual and never overtly showed any sign of being ill. Again I was told about her 'rights' and offered lots of sympathy in the situation. Somehow their sentiments seemed hollow. Surely, the pressures they had heaped on Shelley must have contributed in some way to her deterioration. Should they have allowed someone in her delicate state to work twelve-hour days? Could they not have insisted that she be referred to some medical board for a health check?

We were assured that she undoubtedly had a job when she was discharged. I needed to inform them of her decision not to return and this was greeted with disappointment, although I suspect this was a disguise for utter relief. The problem had been shifted to us. We were assured that wages would follow along with cards, presents and other such signs of goodwill. However, this all left a bitter taste in my mouth and hardness in my heart; they could have done something to help my girl. Just like the gym, they chose to turn a blind eye for their own ends; they did not put Shelley first.

With all the business concluded we made our visit to the hospital. Shelley was on a strict regimen of liquid food supplements and seemed fairly settled, glad that all arrangements had been made and stress removed from her. She was frequently monitored for all the usual stats and blood was taken, with difficulty, every day.

The same pattern of visiting followed on the Tuesday, 2 pm until about 6pm, when Neil would sometimes take over on his way from work.

On Wednesday we had to drive to a garage three miles from our home and pick up a hire vehicle. We had arranged in advance to pick it up, but the first stress came when it wasn't ready! Eventually one was acquired only for us to find that the tail door didn't lock! We were going to empty Shelley's flat and then go to visit her, so her furniture would have to remain in the unlocked van for several hours at the hospital. They had no other van available, so we had to take the chance.

At the flat, we met with a couple of relatives who had come to help with the lifting and the cleaning. We just managed to get it all done by the time the letting agency's representative came. He was quite happy, as everything was immaculate, and was confident that a new tenant would be found quickly. This would mean that Shelley would only lose a month's rent and her bond would be returned.

After a quick bite to eat at a local pub it was off to the hospital again, furniture and all; I know what a snail has to contend with now!

When we returned home, totally exhausted, the van had to be hurriedly emptied into Shelley's old room downstairs and returned. Rick was good, helping to lift, and soon it was mission accomplished. The problem was that Shelley had acquired a flat's worth of furniture now and it was going to be quite a task to fit it all in. That, coupled with Emily's stock of acquisitions ready for her first home in a few months, meant that there was little room for manoeuvring; every available space was filled!

We had tea and Glen was exhausted, falling asleep in the chair; the strain was worse for him because he got all the heavy work to do. He wanted us to go to bed early, ready to face the next day, but I couldn't; there were things I needed to do.

I sat in Shelley's room, on her new settee, thinking of the events of the past six weeks. I had a strong sense of déjà vu; she was back here, where she belonged, or at least her belongings were. This gave me some comfort and a strong sense that I needed to get things right this time. Whatever her future would bring, she needed my total support, even if her plans were contrary to my ideals.

I spent the next few hours patiently trying to arrange the room into a homely sanctuary for her return. I didn't realise then how long I would have to wait or how wonderful that return would be.

CHAPTER XIII

The Fall Before the Rise

Shelley had been in the general hospital for about ten days, I had returned to a typical working pattern, and 'normality' seemed to have become re-established in our lives. After a weekend of visiting, with Shelley on a regimen of supplement drinks four or five times a day and regular monitoring, I set off for my job in school with a lighter heart than of late. The morning passed and it was good to be able to immerse myself once again in helping youngsters with their work. I left at twelve o'clock, returning home for lunch and to prepare for visiting at 3pm. I should have had a feeling of foreboding, shouldn't I? Surely my finely tuned senses should have warned me something was wrong? They didn't; the drive home was pleasant and normal and ill prepared me for the news I was about to receive.

When I arrived home, Glen was suspiciously cheerful and sat me down straight away with a welcome cuppa. Then he dropped the bombshell. Shelley had suffered some kind of collapse and had a few injuries. Apparently the hospital first rang him at about ten o'clock but only got the answerphone, as he was walking the dog. A message was left for him to contact them. At that stage, they thought Shelley had suffered a cardiac arrest and was in danger of dying. By the time he returned the call they were sure she had just fainted and that it was less serious, but we knew she had done some damage.

I was beside myself and flew at Glen for not being there when they rang and for not getting me home from work earlier. I wanted to leave for the hospital immediately. As always, Glen calmed me down and sensibly suggested that as she was now out of danger, we should get some lunch first. I reluctantly agreed but was secretly champing at the bit to make the twenty-mile journey.

I expected to see Shelley with the odd bruise but wasn't prepared for what greeted us. She had a cut all through her eyebrow, which was held together with strips, a bruised and battered face and a damaged front tooth. It was broken in half vertically, the nerve exposed and hanging down like a piece of thread. I can feel you shudder, and even now I go cold at the memory. She had given her usual blood sample to the nurse, who had left, closing the door behind her. Shelley liked the door closed – it shut her away from humanity as far as possible – but I always thought it should have at least been ajar so the nurses at the desk could check on her. After all, most anorexics like secrecy and she needed to be monitored for her own safety.

All Shelley could tell us was that the nurse had left and then some time later she woke up, on the floor, covered in blood. The first the staff knew of it was when they heard her staggering about, trying to get back onto the bed; negligence? I was none too happy, but at least our worst fear had not been realised. Isn't it funny how we sometimes settle for shoddy dealings when in the scheme of things a disaster has been averted? We were just grateful to still have her and it didn't seem important to ask questions.

We cuddled and comforted Shelley, who looked white and shaken and who was clearly in pain from the tooth. We asked the staff for painkillers and enquired as to whether the hospital had a dentist who could come to see her. The answer was a less than helpful 'no'.

After a short sleep, Shelley was brought her drink, chilled, as this was the only way she would have it. When she sipped, the pain through the damaged tooth was dreadful, which was obviously going to add to her reluctance to drink. I mentioned this to the nurses, but got little by way of a caring response. Not everyone regards anorexia as an illness. She brought it on herself, didn't she? Wasn't she therefore reaping her just deserts? I asked if we would be allowed to take her to a nearby dentist but was told that this was not possible either, due to her precarious state. So she (and we) spent several miserable days while she suffered dreadful pain and was still required to drink to gain weight. Progress was slow, about one or two pounds a week if we were lucky.

Finally, after about ten days, we were allowed to take her to a dentist local to the hospital. This meant private treatment, and as she needed cosmetic work it was going to cost a few hundred pounds. After a few calls we found someone able to see her and willing to accept her current health risks.

Shelley got many strange looks as she waited for the

dentist to call her in, and seemed anxious; she was becoming more institutionalised and was ill at ease away from the security of her regular checks. At one point she almost left, but eventually we were seen. Impressions were taken to make a crown and she was fitted with a temporary one. Relieved, we returned her to the hospital. However, after the first sip of her drink through a straw, within an hour of returning, the temporary crown snapped and we were back to the beginning. We then had to wait a few more days to get a return appointment, Shelley suffering in silence all the while.

On the second visit, a better job was done and lasted her until the final fitting. When she returned home, though, there would be many more visits to the dentist, and many more embarrassments when she was minus a front tooth and had to go to work. What kind of hell is the life of an anorexic, and what cruel tricks it plays on the individual's dignity and self-respect.

CHAPTER XIV

When Will It End?

Most people are familiar with the expression 'like watching paint dry' to describe a tedious situation, and Shelley's hospital stay was no different.

Every day, around one, after a morning at work, we would set off for the hospital. We would find Shelley relaxing on her bed, gaunt and lifeless, usually with the television on and the door closed. The room, the whole atmosphere, was airless and suffocating. It was a rare treat if anyone, such as a nurse or cleaner, came in to relieve the monotony. The arrival of the tea trolley was a monumental occasion, and the decision between coffee or hot chocolate had a massive wow factor!

We couldn't go anywhere and it was difficult to know what to say or do. We usually began with kisses and hugs and then made the usual enquiries about how she was and what had happened. Invariably the answers were the same: she was OK (a massive relief) and nothing significant had occurred. As she was only weighed once a week there was little to report in between and we waited with bated breath for Friday to find out if any progress had been made. Shelley was on a regimen of five food supplement drinks per day, which were brought to her at intervals. She would sip them through a straw and each drink could take her up to ninety minutes to finish.

Conversation was difficult. What can you say to someone who is virtually bed-bound and doing nothing that a 'normal' eighteen-year-old should be doing? Our news revolved around work, traffic hold-ups and the pets. Hers was even more stilted, and usually consisted of some overnight drama with an elderly patient or some run-in with a nurse with 'an attitude'.

So the weeks passed. Shelley would drink the supplements and have blood tests daily. Apart from that she seemed to be left to her own devices. Weight gain went on slowly, about one to two pounds per week, although sometimes we would go through a whole week to find she had lost weight again! That was when demoralisation set in for both her and us: another week of all our lives gone, without any progress. These were the really difficult times. She had been 4st 6lb and she needed to get to at least 6st 3lb before the cardiac arrest risk could be removed. With the rate of progress as slow as it was, it was easy to feel desolate.

Sometimes, additional help was offered. She was visited by an eating disorders expert in the beginning, and he tried to find out what had been responsible for her illness and attempted to discuss a recovery plan. It was even suggested that she go to a special clinic, renowned for treating such disorders and highly acclaimed by 'the stars', but to no avail. Shelley was not willing to communicate, cooperate or even be sociable. Anything to do with food or her illness was taboo and any meaningful discussion was vetoed by her. On the rare occasion when we were witness to such meetings we were mortified. We hadn't realised that our normally sweet daughter could be so rude and dismissive. Because of her negative attitude little of merit could be done and it was decided that she should be referred to a dietician and counsellor: decisions which Shelley greeted with disgust. It was not an easy time and her mood swings were horrific. Some days I wanted to leave as soon as I arrived, because no matter how we tried she was determined to be hateful to us. Many times I had to walk away, stamp the corridors, returning for more of the same. It's what you do as a parent, isn't it?

In due course we were told the dietician had paid a visit to see if they could start Shelley on a re-feeding programme with 'proper food', but unfortunately her lack of cooperation led to this being abandoned as an option. Her illness was dictating that she stay with the dark forces and any positive, well-meaning initiative had to be quashed.

One particular day stands out in my memory. We had just arrived for a visit and Shelley's room was empty; she had gone to the toilet. On the bed was a tray of sausages, a jacket potato and beans. I called to the kitchen porter to remove the meal and was told categorically that Shelley had ordered it. It was almost laughable, like some kind of sick joke! Of course it was a mistake; she was a vegetarian and an anorexic; unless a miracle had happened there was no way she would eat a meal like this. Sadly, no change had taken place, it had been an error, but I prayed so fervently that one day she would indeed place such an order for food and then eat it with relish! I will reveal, reader, that my prayers were to be answered, but not for a long time to come.

CHAPTER XV

Rare Insights

On almost every occasion when we arrived for a visit, the television would be on, with cookery programmes being of special interest. It was as if Shelley were somehow feeding on the food she saw. This routine continued for some time after she eventually returned home, conversations being held against the backdrop of the latest 'dishes of the day' created with a few unimpressive ingredients. One particular well-known cookery programme still manages, even now, to evoke memories I would rather forget.

Another trait anorexics have is to trawl food displays in shops, again compelled by some obsessive Antichrist, bent on admiring, touching but never sampling the food they see. My experience with Shelley has made me notice this same behaviour in others with the illness. It's like some *Ancient Mariner* connection, where the thing that haunts them is the one thing they won't allow themselves to have, and they seem unable to free themselves from the destructive cycle.

Not all visits were bad. Sometimes we would play Scrabble or cards, and Shelley seemed to enjoy such times of camaraderie. We also tried to introduce hobbies that would while the days away. On one occasion Shelley made lots of wool wristbands which the nurses bought for a few pence. I even commissioned her to do a batch for pupils at a school I was in, and I gave them out as little Easter presents. They had a special significance because these children knew my daughter was in hospital and often asked how she was, so the bands were received with understanding of their importance.

Visits continued in the same vein, with us visiting on weekdays and Saturdays and Neil in the evenings and on Sunday. Emily was marvellous during this period. She gave up her valuable time on weekends to visit her sister, spoil her with gifts and wheel her around in the wheelchair, brightening her days with tales of the outside world. It was obvious to see how much she missed her sister and the close, loving relationship they had enjoyed prior to her illness.

As Shelley's weight slowly increased, we were allowed to take her down to the cafeteria, or into the garden in her wheelchair. This was a major development and lifted her, and our, spirits no end. She could see life, smell flowers, go to the shop and get the so-important fresh air. Sometimes on a fine day we would 'escape', pushing her around the perimeter of the hospital grounds and getting away from just staring at the buildings and 'inmates'. We began to feel hopeful again, alive, normal even, and were encouraged by the fact that the stares became fewer as Shelley looked better.

During these happier times, it was put to Shelley that she consider seeing a counsellor to try to ascertain the reason for her illness, as she maintained she was not aware of what had caused it. She did not want to see the hospital counsellor, so Emily arranged a visit from a counsellor through her employers. Shelley requested that I be present for the visit. The counsellor was a lovely lady, very discreet and not at all pushy, and Shelley talked easily enough but not about anything of real significance. When a follow-up was suggested the shutters came down again, and the woman was told, like all the other professionals, that Shelley didn't need help and would sort things out for herself.

A short time afterwards, I tackled the subject again. I told Shelley that I had seen a counsellor a couple of times prior to her hospitalisation because I was not coping well. I told her that my own counsellor had suggested writing down key events in my life, happy and sad, to create talking points and possibly uncover things that were more important than I realised. I asked Shelley to consider doing this but with little conviction that she would.

I was proved wrong and on the next visit was handed two A4 pages of neat, miniscule notes ordered around a brainstorming approach. Topics included holidays, rows, health, her birth father, weddings, death, college and love. I was encouraged, gaining new insight into what had troubled her in her life. I believe these feelings were fundamental to her illness and indeed to many anorexics to some degree or another.

Many of the notes dealt with self-perception and low self-esteem. She seemed haunted by the opinions of others and fearful of the impact of her actions on others.

She showed her sensitivity, fearful of being hurt by others and yet not wanting to hurt others herself. She also admitted to a very strong pride, which prevented her from acknowledging error. U-turns were not in her repertoire, although she also admitted that she dearly wanted to say, 'I'm wrong, I'm sorry, please help me.'

However, the revelation that struck me as the most relevant was the admission that she needed to feel different from her twin sister, a special individual in her own right, worthy of particular attention. She cited a memory that when she was five, she was diagnosed with a heart murmur which her sister didn't have. She said the problem made her feel individual and special, and she remembered her sister crying because she couldn't have an ECG done as well!

During Shelley's hospital stay Emily had begun to comment that no one was interested in her, only her sister, so we had to try to make her the priority too sometimes. The whole twin thing is complex: two people, genetically identical but intellectually individual. Certainly, many of Shelley's problems seemed to stem from the time she left secondary school and made different choices to her sister. Had she envied Emily her choices, the freedom, the boyfriend? Had she regretted her own choices, with the pride she had mentioned preventing her from backtracking or making changes? I don't know if any of us will ever really know, but it takes a lot of courage in life to say, 'I'm unhappy and I'm going to change direction.' I wonder if the famous line 'to thine own self be true' is not the real recipe for happiness.

Shelley had been in hospital since February and it was now the end of May. She was getting restless, but still the 'safe' weight had not been reached. One sunny day we negotiated taking her out for a ride in the car and were told this was all right as long as she took her drinks with her. We sat outside a pub, me, Glen, Emily and Shelley, on the canal bank, and we seemed almost like a family again, but not quite. We sipped lager and Shelley sat in a big coat sipping her life-juice, but it's surprising how little you settle for in the face of tragedy.

Another time we were allowed to bring Shelley home for a few hours. She saw her 'stuff' set up in her room and seemed pleased, but you could also see the sadness and regret and sense her thoughts of failure. Like a lot of 'institutionalised' people she seemed to want to return to the security of hospital again, but with the reassurance that she would soon be home for good.

The last couple of weeks in hospital were the hardest. The last few pounds wouldn't seem to go on, and in fact on one occasion we learned she had lost weight again. We were despondent and so were the staff. An extra drink was introduced but to no avail; the weight would just not go on. It was June now and the girls' birthday was coming up, and Shelley was adamant that she would be out of hospital by then. But still the weight hovered on the brink!

We were baffled and so were the nurses. A suggestion was made that Shelley was not having all her drinks. At my peril I questioned her on this, and she was affronted that we would think she needed to be asked. I told the nurses so, but still they weren't convinced. As a result Shelley had to be supervised while she took her drinks and in rebellion took about two hours to drink each small carton. It was embarrassing and didn't work in the end, because the staff would be called away for more pressing duties and this defeated the whole exercise. It was only a couple of years ago that Shelley admitted to me that she hadn't been taking all of her drinks. Obviously the staff knew more than I did from previous experience with eating disorders.

After one particularly depressing visit when no weight had been gained and Glen, Shelley and I had had to attend a meeting to discuss a plan of action, Shelley wrote me this letter.

Dear Mum,
I just wanted to say a big thank you to you for helping me through the meeting and cheering me up on Friday – I couldn't have got through it by myself.

I still feel really disappointed but in the long term it might speed things up if I spend as much time as possible resting in hospital. I'm sorry that it hasn't been much fun for you and Glen coming to see me this week, I'll try and make up for it next week. You've been so great to me, and all the nurses keep saying I'll be alright because they have noticed how close a family we are, and how caring and supportive you and Glen are.

Your idea of writing things down has been the

biggest help (including that of the nurses) that anyone has given me – it makes me feel much more secure about coming home because I know I can talk to any of you if things get on top of me, and I know that you'll make sure that I don't slip back down.

This last 8/9 months has been the hardest I have ever been through and it takes a lot of work to keep going sometimes, but as time goes on I feel that I am gradually beating my problem and feel like I am achieving my goal of being well again.

Although it has been hard for us all, one good thing that has come out of my being ill is that I feel so much closer to you, Glen, Emily and all the family than I ever have done, and when I come out of hospital, I'm looking forward to doing more things as a family and to sharing more hugs with you.

I know I'm not the best at showing my feelings but you're the most important and special person in my life, and I can never thank you enough for all that you've done for me. You've done more for me than I could ever wish for. You should be really proud of yourself for what a beautiful person you are – inside and out. I hope that as I get older I can be more selfless like you are.

You're my best friend and you always will be. I need you and Glen so much right now and I always will. I'm just so sorry to have put you through all of this trouble and inconvenience – you don't deserve it.

I really enjoyed sitting out in the sun with you yesterday – my room looks lovely with my lovely plants and groovy balloons!
Take care, love you loads and loads,
Shelley xxxxxxxxx

This letter gave us hope that she wanted to get better; in it we glimpsed the old Shelley, the sweet, caring girl. It seemed to focus her. A couple of weeks later she had made her 'safe weight' and, music to our ears, she was coming home after four and a half months in hospital. I have to admit to some apprehension because she would be our responsibility again and her weight still had to be steadily increased, but the relief at not having to visit the hospital any more was enormous. She would be home in time for her nineteenth birthday; what a celebration that would be!

CHAPTER XVI

Back to Normality

I cannot begin to express our feelings of joy and relief at having Shelley home with us again. No longer did we have to face the tedious journeys to the hospital, the strained visiting sessions and the 'drip-fed' weight gain. Now that she was home we would be able to make her well again and encourage her, in our own ways, to return to her former self.

It was a fine theory, but reality was a different story. Life was in fact far from perfect. Shelley continued to have her supplements and we allowed her to self-govern in this quarter, but her mood and integration into the family unit did not improve. We put this down to an adjustment period and were quietly confident that things would become better.

The transition was probably harder for Shelley because her sister Emily moved into her first home with her long-standing boyfriend, Kev, a week after Shelley came out of hospital. Not the best of timings, but she had her own life to lead. Increasingly we had sensed that Emily felt left out and suffocated by all the emphasis on Shelley, so we hoped the move would give her space, a new focus and a sense of importance, even though secretly we felt nineteen was too young. I now know that Emily had been finding things harder than we imagined and was annoyed at everyone's time being absorbed by Shelley, even though her sister continued to be the most important person in her life; quite a paradox, but understandable. We supported Emily in her move and helped with decorating. Secretly, however, we believed Shelley felt envious, further reminded that she had 'messed up'. This possibly explained her difficulty in settling back at home.

As I was now on school holidays I began my usual spring cleaning and gardening tasks, occasionally trying to involve Shelley, but to no avail. She spent most days in her room watching TV, mostly cookery programmes, hardly venturing out, and evenings were spent with Neil. I had hoped for a new understanding, a new closeness, but it wasn't there; I felt like a stranger in my own home, not a feeling I enjoyed. There was an atmosphere, but I couldn't gauge what it was or why it was there. So the days continued, with no real progress being made.

The girls' birthday came and the family assembled, but it was tense and awkward. Shelley would eat and drink nothing, not even the cake I had specially made, but I told myself that at least she was alive to see it and to spend it at home. You learn to be grateful and to thank God for even the smallest of mercies.

Two weeks after Shelley came home, we had to return to the hospital for her official dismissal meeting. Glen and I attended, along with Shelley, Neil, the psychiatric team (about five people) and the staff nurse responsible for Shelley's care. It started well enough, with them checking on her progress and confirming that her weight had remained steady, and then events rapidly went downhill. When questioned about how things were going Shelley launched into a personal attack on me, saying that I was constantly plaguing her about taking her drinks and that I wouldn't leave her in peace. I was stunned. I hadn't seen this coming! I retaliated, saying that what she was accusing me of was just not true; I was working until one o'clock every day and then had all my chores, and anyway the circumstances of her enforced exile to her room did not encourage such interference on my part. Shelley continued to launch her attack and I continued to appeal to the team and could not believe it when they just sat there, nonchalantly, making no comments at all. I couldn't cope; why would no one believe that all I had done was carry on as normally as possible, allowing Shelley to adjust? I broke down and said I could no longer stay and listen to such lies, fleeing to a side room to sob and shake my head with disbelief. Why was Shelley doing this to me; what had I done?

Glen came after me and persuaded me, against my better judgement, to return, and the meeting was concluded. Shelley had to sign an action document agreeing to continue with her drinks and attend an outpatient clinic at a local mental health establishment. Glen, Neil and I were made guardians of the contract and could contact the team at any time with concerns or if Shelley's condition worsened. There seemed to be some solace in this.

I escaped the meeting as quickly as I could, disgusted that these health experts didn't believe me, and leant against a wall in the corridor, trying to compose myself. I was completely drained and felt desolate, so it was utterly incongruous when, a few minutes later, Shelley emerged with Neil, thanked us for coming and told us, in an upbeat tone, that she and Neil were going off to do some shopping now and would see us later at home. I even got a hug and kiss, not received well at the time! It was as if the person in the meeting had been someone else, an alter ego. Welcome to the double life of the anorexia sufferer!

There is an old saying that when your children are young they make your arms ache, and when they are older they make your heart ache. The truth of this felt very real following the meeting. A mother's love is, of course, unconditional, and we learn to grow thick skins when necessary! Once again I looked for reasons to excuse Shelley's behaviour, and I felt that her current inactivity and lack of job were partly to blame. She felt different, 'freakish', and longed to return to normality, but with no real idea of how to achieve this.

Whilst in hospital Shelley had read a lot of popular magazines, especially the ones that sensationalise real-life stories in a bid to boost sales. One day she announced that she was thinking of writing about her anorexia experience in a bid to earn some money, as it was promised that you could earn up to £600 for just a few hundred words. We thought the experience of writing her thoughts down was positive anyway, and if it was printed then that would be an added bonus. At last she had something to focus on, and maybe if she did reach print her experiences might help some other sufferers.

The whole operation was 'cloak and dagger' and we

were told very little until she announced that she had been asked to send in some photographs of her and Neil. Shortly afterwards she was told she would be in print and the excitement was enormous. She wasn't paid the £600 she had hoped for but was pleased to make print and receive almost £300.

When I read the article I was slightly shocked by some of the 'media language' and Shelley said her words had been tweaked here and there, but overall the message was much as she had portrayed it. What I wasn't prepared for was the amount of publicity Shelley's plight got as a result of the article, with people stopping both her and me saying they had read it and how awful the experience must have been. Although it had started as a monetary pursuit, her work had caused a stir and created awareness, with a wider impact than we could ever have imagined. Here was something positive; would this spur her on to greater things?

Later in the month Glen and I decided to attend a meeting for anorexics, bulimics and their carers, which the eating disorder team had made us aware of. We tried to persuade Shelley to attend with us, but she wouldn't.

We entered the crowded room with some trepidation, trying to work out who fell into which categories. Most were sufferers of bulimia and on the surface looked relatively healthy, but then our first anorexic arrived and there was no identity crisis. She was thin and waif-like, wanted to be noticed by the whole room, and insisted on walking in bare-footed and sitting curled up on a chair. I immediately spotted the attention-seeking behaviour, the wasted body, and my heart went out to her.

Before the meeting we struck up a conversation with her and explained we were there as observers, as parents of an anorexic. She was immediately interested in our relationship with Shelley and said she had moved away and did not get on with her parents, a fact she was obviously troubled by. The same old patterns we had experienced, so perhaps it wasn't our fault after all. She also acknowledged that her family troubles were of her making and that she wasn't proud of the wedge her illness had driven between herself and her family. Her pain was almost tangible; we wanted to be able to help her and she us. She said that Shelley was lucky that we were bearing with her, even when times were really bad.

The lectures started and we learned all about eating disorders, their effect on the body and how health can be restored with proper help. We broke for lunch and went to the local sandwich bar, passing our anorexic friend, foodless, who was heading off to the shops, a long walk away, obviously sticking to the ritual exercising.

After a few more sessions we returned home, laden with lots of leaflets, some enlightenment, but mostly depression. We had been told the good, the bad and the ugly, but nowhere was the leaflet on how to persuade your child to get the help they need, how to cross the great barrier and arrive in Healthy Land again. As always, it was up to the person concerned to seek the help they needed when they got desperate enough, leaving their loved ones to hope that they didn't die on the way. Once again we felt helpless; only Shelley could make herself well!

CHAPTER XVII

New Frontiers

September was a difficult month. I had just returned to my job in a local school and Shelley to her bedroom exile, spending many hours alone. She needed to get out, socialise, find a job, but none of this seemed to be forthcoming. She made applications but became despondent every time she heard nothing, convinced she was 'useless' and 'of no value'. Depression seemed to be setting in, and I am sure she was lapsing on taking her supplements because she was losing weight and her moods were deteriorating.

After a time, I became increasingly anxious, afraid for her state of mind and fearful she would do something silly. In desperation I called the eating disorders consultant and asked his advice. He paid Shelley a visit, got open hostility, and concluded that she needed to return to hospital. I said we would consider it and let him know our decision, even though he really wanted to arrange things then and there.

During lots of discussion and soul-searching, Shelley pleaded with us not to admit her again, promising she would do whatever we wanted to set things right. I knew she needed help, knew she needed to regain weight, but wasn't convinced myself that hospital was the correct option. I told Shelley I would fight her corner and keep her out of committal, but only if she agreed to keep certain rules that we would mutually compile. A soft option for her? No, because I promised to admit her immediately if she reneged on any of the agreed steps. Of course we had to be realistic; the steps had to be achievable and not too ambitious.

Mercifully, the possibility of rehospitalisation was enough of a threat to keep her on the straight and narrow. The eating disorder team thought I was wrong, but I felt that I had to try a new, more proactive approach this time, if only to satisfy myself that it was viable. We had passed another milestone and for the moment, at least, things began to improve again.

A couple of weeks later, Shelley succeeded in gaining a part-time job on the tills at a supermarket a few miles away. The change was immediate. She had something to get up for, the all-important remuneration, which in turn gave her independence, and there was a real boost to her self-esteem. It also put some distance between us and, as a result, relationships improved. She seemed to enjoy the work, especially meeting people, and everyone said what a lovely girl she was, customers and staff alike. Amazingly she seemed to cope well with the exertion of the job and her confidence grew in leaps and bounds. I worked in the same town and so called in to shop occasionally and see how she was. Encouragingly, this was always well received, and I felt we were getting back to how we were.

One day she came home quite concerned. Apparently a customer had been going through the till and Shelley had noticed, while packing her bags, that she had lots of 'ready meals'. The customer must have felt conscious of this because she had commented that she was currently visiting her daughter in hospital and didn't have time to cook. She had confided that her daughter was suffering from anorexia, and Shelley had been very sympathetic. The same shopper returned to her till several days later and Shelley asked for a progress report. Gradually they built a relationship, with the woman being glad of someone to talk to and realising Shelley was a fellow sufferer.

A month or so later, the customer told Shelley that her daughter was now home but she feared she might lapse into her old ways. Shelley said she could possibly help. That night she asked if we minded her giving the woman the self-help package we had brought back from the meeting we attended. It was for her, we had never seen her read it or practise its principles, but here she was ready to try to help someone else. Irony of ironies! Shelley was always the champion of a good cause, an admirable quality, but seemed unable to grasp the seriousness of her own need. We learned afterwards that the woman had passed the pack on and her daughter seemed to be making progress – another example of Shelley's beautiful and selfless nature.

October signalled my fiftieth birthday. *Oh no! Not another birthday!* I hear you cry. I have to say these were my sentiments exactly. Everyone was saying it was special and that I should celebrate in style, but somehow it seemed incongruous with how I was feeling. Until Shelley was well I felt I would never really be alive again. It was surreal, like existing but on some parallel plane. I felt slightly robotic, performing the duties I was expected to perform but somehow removed from the emotions associated with them. Just as a hedgehog hibernates to avoid the cold, shutting down as many bodily functions as possible, so it is when you are hurting deep inside: you need to shut down, shut out dangers and encase yourself in some protective shell so you can't be hurt, at least for the foreseeable future or until the hurt is removed.

With the birthday looming a compromise was reached and a family meal arranged at a local pub. 'Family' here was the family minus Shelley and Neil; they would not be attending. I had learned to accept the situation, but it still hurt; after all, you only become fifty once and you can never regain the moment.

Understandably, emotions ran high on the actual day. Shelley had to go to work but gave me a beautiful card, and shortly before she left the doorbell rang and I got the most wonderful bouquet of roses from her and Emily. A photograph was taken and I looked about one hundred! The emotion was too much after the experiences of the last year.

The rest of the day was very enjoyable. Emily made it special by coming to visit and bringing another beautiful card, telling me I would get the family gift later. Glen had arranged a weekend away and a theatre visit to see *Joseph*, also buying me a pretty gold bangle-watch. He made up for my hurts, was always there, my mainstay.

We assembled for the meal at about seven o'clock, all in our birthday best! The mood was good but muted. Someone important was missing. Imagine my shock and pleasure when Shelley arrived, still in shop uniform, to wish me well and to say she hoped we enjoyed our meal. I still have a wonderful photograph of my two beautiful daughters flanking me and smiling widely. You've guessed it; it made my day! Shortly afterwards she disappeared, like some Cinderella figure who wasn't allowed to stay at the ball, but the 'glass slipper' gesture was unforgettable.

As I write I feel very conscious of the parable of the prodigal son, sensing how difficult all the focus on Shelley must have been for Emily. Emily had always tried hard to please, had never disappointed, but seemed to be in the shadow of her sister. I don't think I appreciated, or even now fully appreciate, how difficult life had become for her. She didn't deserve to be lost in her sister's problems or to be seen as any less important, but I fear this was how she perceived the situation. So maybe now is a good time to acknowledge her patience, suffering and fortitude, and to remind her that she was always loved equally – however unapparent it may have seemed at times.

The rest of the evening was excellent. Good food, good company, including Emily and partner Kev, my stepson Rick and both sets of parents. Glen had organised a wonderful cake decorated with a deer and a robin, two of my favourite creatures, and the 'kids' had bought me a gold rope necklace which I loved. As recent birthdays had gone, this was a good one. I can almost hear your sigh of relief!

Had we broken the mould? Was the future on the up? Well, reader, apart from a few bad moments, I can safely say I believe this day signalled new beginnings for us all.

PART III
The Rebuild

CHAPTER XVIII

A Closeness Begins

About a month after my birthday, Shelley announced that she was moving into a rented flat with Neil. I welcomed the news. It would only be ten minutes away and was a fresh start for both of them, with privacy to build on and restore their relationship. Glen and I happily helped with the cleaning and moving, as did Neil's parents. Of course we were all apprehensive, knowing we would not be able to monitor the situation quite so easily, but we were pleased that at last they felt ready to set up home together.

The flat was in a central position over a Chinese restaurant and, apart from when the New Year celebrations kicked in and the dragon was paraded, it proved to be a fairly peaceful location. They had a large sitting room, two bedrooms etc. and furnished it tastefully and comfortably. There was room to spread out if they needed to, and the atmosphere was calm and happy.

When Christmas Eve arrived we were asked along for a drink and mince pies. They had a large tree, lovingly decorated, and seemed very happy. It was a relief to us all, especially as Shelley seemed well and her weight stable.

This oasis of calm continued for about six months, during which time Shelley secured a much better job, administration with a local college. Her improved financial security meant she and Neil could now consider buying their first property. Finding something they could afford was not easy, but eventually they came across a one-bedroomed house in a quiet cul-de-sac. It was compact but charming, with enough room for essential needs but small enough to maintain.

Moving house is always stressful, but more so when you are mentally vulnerable, as Shelley still was at this time. As the moving date approached the tension began to soar. Shelley was panicking because she had given notice to the owner of her current flat but still had no final moving-in date. Stress was visibly building and there were glimpses of her former self.

Anxious that she should not regress, I suggested they leave the flat anyway at the end of the notice period and move back home until they could take possession of their new house. Finding room for Shelley was not quite as simple as before because we had converted her old downstairs bedroom to a sitting room and Rick was still living at home, but determination has a way of finding a solution against the odds. Shelley and Neil moved into the small bedroom, managing with a single bed and sofa bed. We designated one of the two sitting rooms for their exclusive use, and the rest of their possessions filled up the garage, sheds and various orifices around the house. Pickfords had nothing on us!

To begin with things were OK, with Shelley and Neil at work during the day and free to see to themselves when they came home. Gradually, however, the old tensions began to mount, increased by the ever-lengthening wait for a completion date. With the tension came the mood swings and ultimately the arguments.

I remember one evening when Glen and I had been to a local theatre. We had given Shelley space all evening, returning about ten o'clock, slightly peckish. I went through to the kitchen to get a dish of cereal and unceremoniously plonked myself on a sofa in 'their' lounge for the few minutes it would take me to eat. I was totally unprepared for the verbal attack that was launched upon me and felt like an intruder in my own house. It hurt and seemed so unfair in the face of all the personal sacrifices and accommodating behaviour we were demonstrating. It reminded me that the old illness still lurked behind the polite facade, waiting to pounce when one little chink breached our agreed wall of protocol. It reminded me too, much to my shame now, of how glad I was when Shelley lived elsewhere and took her illness with her!

Finally, the moving day came and Shelley and Neil moved in with the help of Emily and Kev; we weren't needed. As always, when everything was perfect, we were duly invited for a visit. To be fair, the house was lovely: cosy, stylish and obviously their pride and joy. I had never expected Shelley to realise such an ambition in light of how dire her health had been, and my heart swelled with pride and love. She now lived quite close to Emily, and they began to see more of each other and resume their close relationship.

On the girls' twenty-first birthday in June 2004, Shelley announced that she and Neil had set a date for their wedding, the following February, and handed out the invites. If I'm honest, I had mixed feelings. Of course I was happy about the wedding and wished them well, but my pride, as mother, was severely dented as I hadn't been party to any of the arrangements.

As usual my heart, not my head, ruled my body; I was making judgements before I had all the facts. I tried to conceal it, but I felt as though the final act to hurt me had taken place. I now know I was selfish and wrong and that I should have trusted my intelligent daughter to make sound decisions, following serious thought.

I wanted them to have a church wedding, followed by reception at a hotel, but it was to be a civil wedding at a local golf club. Some time afterwards, when I was more open to reason, Shelley explained that they had chosen the venue to make it easier for Neil's father, who had sadly lost part of a leg through severe diabetes, at only fifty-nine. The golf club had good disabled access and facilities. What an utter idiot I felt. Also, they had kept the numbers small, a smattering of family, friends and associates from work and hobbies, because they intended to pay for everything themselves. A parent's dream scenario!

I had been short-sighted; was this my problem? Had I worked hard all my life to raise two beautiful, intelligent, independent daughters, only to become offended when they decided to draw on the strengths I had fostered? I was in undiscovered territory; it was my turn to feel vulnerable. Perhaps I needed to rethink my strategies; I was dealing with adults now and had to revise how I coped with the change.

Shelley had even thought about the situation of having 'two fathers' (her own dad and her stepdad, Glen) and had decided that both would walk her down the aisle. What a sensitive, caring girl she was.

About two months later, after the dust had settled, I accompanied Shelley to the city hospital for an ultrasound scan. She had been born with a hole in the heart, accompanied by a heart murmur, and this had only been detected on her pre-school check. Whilst in hospital, now an adult, she had been deemed to need further investigation, just to check no major changes had taken place since her early years. It would also be reassuring to know that no serious damage had been done by the anorexia. Many weeks later we found out all was well.

After the hospital visit we decided to look around a few bridal shops. I remember well the pouring rain, us dashing through the door of Kind Hearts and Coronets, looking like drowned rats, and Shelley unsuitably dressed to 'try on' in jeans and heavy trainers! I am sure the owner thought we had just come in to shelter from the deluge. Eventually, we convinced her we were genuine, and she proved to be a godsend. She was patient with Shelley, who only tried two dresses on; she had fallen in love with the one in the window, and so had I. It was slim-fitting, flaring at the bottom, and had attractive red lacing all down the back. The front was decorated with red and clear beads and crystals, hand-sewn, and I cried when I saw Shelley model it. She looked like a fragile doll and so beautiful, my only concern being the thinness of her arms as it was a sleeveless bodice style.

Shelley said she was unsure, so we decided to go for a coffee and a chat and return later, the assistant reminding us that it would take three months to order; the wedding was in four! Over a single coffee (mine), Shelley confided that she loved the dress but thought it too expensive, but I soon assured her that I would help her to have her fairy-tale dress. We had no chequebook between us, so I went to the bank and drew the deposit in cash, telling Shelley to try the dress again. If she decided it was the one then we could order; otherwise, I would just re-deposit the money in the bank. After precisely ten minutes the dress was decided upon, along with a beautiful tiara; the wedding of the year was on its way!

Sadly, the preparations were to be overshadowed by the unexpected death of Neil's father in December, two months prior to the wedding. He would be robbed of the privilege of seeing his youngest son marry his sweetheart. Or would he? We are all sure his presence was with us on the day, and that he witnessed the wedding that took place against all the odds.

CHAPTER XIX

A Fairytale Wedding

The night before the wedding, in February, Shelley brought her dress to our house, as she wanted to leave for the ceremony from her old home. She was clutching a bag and said I was to stow it with all her other things and was not to look, as it was a surprise for tomorrow. I had my suspicions and hopes, but somehow managed not to betray her trust and take a sneak preview!

A couple of hours later, Shelley, Emily and I met to go for our 'hen night.' We had all had acrylic nails and for once I felt I had a lady's hands, even if I couldn't drive the car or open doors! Having never had them before, I hoped I would be more manually dextrous by the next day, as at this moment I would have needed dressing, never mind the bride!

Our party was a quiet affair. Shelley wore a pink veil and L plates, and we sat before a nice fire in a favourite local pub. It lasted about ninety minutes and then Shelley wanted to go home. With no real chance to eat or drink it was probably just as well. When Glen arrived to drop us home, he, Emily and I went for a final drink together, pondering how the next day would go and whether there would be any drama.

Saturday arrived, a lovely, blustery sunny day, despite it

being winter. We had decorated the railings outside with wedding banners and a few balloons; spirits were optimistic. Shelley turned up, happy and smiling, and the preparations for the day began. As the wedding was not until three we seemed to have time to take things at a leisurely pace.

We felt we had already had our share of drama. On the Wednesday Glen had had his hired morning suit delivered, only to discover it was too small and too short in the sleeve, even though he had been measured. We had said nothing to Shelley for fear of causing unnecessary stress, instead arranging with the hire company to get a replacement, which we would pick up on the Thursday evening, a journey of twenty-plus miles. All seemed to be straightforward, then on the Thursday evening we had a call from Shelley's dad. He wanted to call by to collect his suit from us on the way to his hotel. He turned up with his wife, and I felt most inhospitable not offering a coffee or a sit-down, but we didn't want to reveal that we needed to change Glen's suit in case it got back to Shelley and upset her. So we waffled about some prior commitment, gave him his suit and bade them farewell until the next day.

The first people to arrive on the wedding day were the hair and beauty team. Shelley (the bride!) had refused to have her hair or face done from the offset, but Emily and I obliged. We were pleased with the results and opened the champagne to get in the mood.

Then the tension began to build. Shelley's dad and Rick arrived to decorate the cars, as they were using their own, and we began to get ready. Shelley had no urgency about her and time was getting short. Emily and I got ready and went to help Shelley. She began by wearing a black-and-white chequered bra under her dress and it just didn't go. I asked her why she wasn't wearing her new cream one; of course it was too big. I suggested that the straps wouldn't look right as they showed, and I was snapped at before she agreed to tuck them in. Then, because I was feeling upset, I couldn't manage to lace her into her dress, so Glen came to the rescue – good, calm, solid Glen!

I returned upstairs to a vision of beauty. Shelley looked resplendent in her beautiful dress, her hair in place and no make-up. She had donned her 'surprise' now, a white fur stole, and she looked like a fragile snow maiden. The thinness of her arms was hidden and she was perfect. She clutched her bouquet of red silk roses with ivory ribbon and looked ready to face the world. I looked from her to Emily, dressed in a burgundy gown with a tiara and carrying ivory roses, and felt I would burst. This was what all the pain was about twenty-one years ago, to give life and breath to two beautiful daughters, who had never disappointed, never failed me, and who, in spite of what we had been through, would always be most precious to me. Determination set in. No one and nothing would spoil this day; my princess would have her fairytale wedding.

I know also that Glen and Shelley's dad were both stunned when they saw her, shedding a few tears, both proud of her in their own ways.

Shelley was to travel in her dad's car with Glen, as they

were both giving her away, and Emily and I were being driven by Rick. A few neighbours had assembled to watch her leave, but then the unthinkable happened: the wind blew, the heavens opened and the mild sunny day turned hateful. We had to run for the cars to preserve Shelley's dress and our hairdos!

Rick's car was pointing down the road and Shelley's up. Shelley left first, and we assumed her dad would turn the car around and follow us; it was the most direct route. Instead they went up the road, parked, and waited for us to follow them; it was just like a slapstick comedy. You've guessed it: we waited in Rick's car for them to come and they waited in their car for us to come. We tried to ring on the mobile, but they had it switched off.

In the end, due to time restraints, I decided they must have gone on, knowing that Glen knew how to get there, so we should do the same. We set off, balloons flapping, and soon, when the windscreen wipers had to be used, got the ribbons caught up. Emily, in the front, had to reach out and grab the ribbons to keep them clear. We were all laughing and giggling and without a care in the world.

We pulled into the car park from one direction, and Shelley from the other. At least we were at the 'church' on time! We were immediately directed to an area for some pre-wedding photographs, still tense from the travel mix-up, and it took a few moments to relax again. But, hey, isn't this the stuff of weddings? You need a blip or two to keep you on your toes.

The service went well except for one further drama.

Kev had recorded some music for the entry, but for some reason, when Neil played it, it wouldn't work. So a few minutes prior to the service Neil was rummaging through mates' cars trying to find suitable CDs!

I believe Shelley entered to Phil Collins instead of Michael Jackson, but I don't think anyone noticed. She was walked down the aisle by two very tense dads but looked calm and regal. The nans were crying and I was blubbing, even though I had said I wouldn't. I don't remember much else about the ceremony, I was too emotional, but about twenty minutes later Shelley and Neil were united, a team, ready to face a new life together and, I prayed, new health as well in Shelley's case.

The reception went well with a nice buffet, lots of wine and champagne, and short-but-sweet speeches. Shelley's dad went up in my estimation when he acknowledged Glen for bringing Shelley up. Past differences behind us, we were united in wishing our daughter and son-in-law every happiness.

Wedding cakes were handed out; Shelley had made her own individual cakes, plain sponges with silver hearts and chocolate sponges with gold hearts, all in silver and gold cases. People liked the novel idea and took the hearts home as souvenirs. Most people stayed the night at the hotel, so we could afford to have a few drinks and dances.

The next day we assembled for breakfast and then waved the happy couple off as they returned home. Glen and I would be picking them up in the early hours of Sunday morning to take them to the airport. Our wedding present had been a week in the Dominican Republic.

Suddenly, everything was over. All the planning and all the stress were gone. Shelley had a new person to be responsible for her now; I had to step back. Could I do it? Cold reality struck and it was both frightening and a big relief. I wondered if Neil, in his new role, would be able to restore Shelley's health, which I had been unable to do. If I'm honest, I didn't think he was strong enough to do it. He loved her, adored her, but could he go against his softer side and be tough for her sake? Only time would tell.

I handed Shelley a letter at the airport and asked her to read it on the plane. I basically told her how much I loved her and how proud of her achievements I was. I said she always succeeded in what she set her mind to, and challenged her to try to beat her illness with the same earnestness. I also acknowledged Neil and his new status in her life, showing, I hope, that I realised my role had changed.

Imagine how I then felt, a week later, when Shelley and Neil emerged from the arrivals lounge at Manchester airport. She was tanned, smiling and looking full in the face. I thought all my prayers had been answered, only to have my hopes dashed when she said she had a swollen face from an allergy to coconut milk. Apparently she had collapsed on the beach on the last day of the holiday and had to be stretchered off! But they were happy, buzzing with memories and intent on getting a dog. An all-inclusive holiday had still resulted in no eating; would anything?

CHAPTER XX

A Happy Ending?

As I write this chapter, it has been almost six years since that fateful birthday when I first noticed Shelley's illness and the devastation it had caused to her body. It has taken me this long to be strong enough to write about my experiences without too much pain.

Why did I decide to write her story? I hoped that by raising awareness of the horrors of anorexia and sharing our experiences, maybe in some small way I would be able to help either a sufferer or their family realise that they are not a freak, are not alone, and are gripped by one of the most truly horrific illnesses. I knew from the onset that my story would offer no answers, little hope, only shared common ground, but I know from personal experience that anorexia is a lonely illness, a misunderstood illness, one which drives a wedge through firm foundations and solid relationships. I wanted to say it's all right to be angry, upset and ignorant, but I also earnestly wanted to say that it is *not* all right to stop loving, to stop caring or to turn a blind eye. Sufferers need love, support, kindness – however difficult to give – and their needs must always come first. Sometimes their lives need saving and you have to be strong enough to do it, even if it comes at personal cost. To sum up, you need to do whatever it takes, and you will be given the strength to do it.

A gloomy picture of a hopeless cause: that's what Shelley's was, wasn't it? No solutions, no future, just an existence, like a weak shadow at evening, present but only just. Depressing reading, isn't it? This was how my story would end, and I feared my daughter would never be well again in my lifetime. Being alive at all and a 'safe weight' was as good as it got – that is, until I got my miracle, at a time when God thought it right.

Now I can finish my account with hope for the future and hope for other sufferers; I can change my ending to a happy one. I am privileged to narrate the events that restored Shelley and have given us hope, God willing, that her future life will be happy and healthy.

The Easter period after the wedding saw Shelley at a low again. She had lost weight, had difficulty taking supplements and was very depressed. We decided we needed to step in and suggest she get help. Now was the time to be proactive and direct, not to sneak behind her back or mutter about her. We told her we had concerns and suggested meeting at a time convenient to her and Neil. We also suggested we involve Neil's mum as an interested party. We were told Good Friday at 6pm would be convenient.

On arrival we were told we would have a fish shop meal and orders were taken, thus eroding some of our meeting time. Eventually, when we did talk, we expressed our concerns, suggested Shelley needed to start her supplements again and offered our support. She was very tearful, Neil became quite aggressive in her defence and as usual I came out as the villain, very upset and drained. I so needed to be close to Shelley and I needed her to be close to me, but we couldn't quite get there. To my shame I was too frightened of a rebuff to pursue the benefits that could have ensued if I had only been braver. But I had done my duty as a parent, offend or please. Fortunately, the advice was taken on board and a significant improvement came about.

This was to remain the pattern as time went on. Shelley would plummet, we would intervene, she would rally and so life continued, until a year ago. Emily was asked what she would like to do for her birthday and said that there wasn't much point having a family meal because Shelley wouldn't have anything. I felt sorry for Emily; she was the forgotten one in the equation. I felt I needed to tell Shelley what Emily had said, so at least she would know how her sister was feeling.

Being honest and telling Shelley that she was not just affecting herself seemed to register. She agreed to try to make a family meal, where she would eat, a future goal, and Glen suggested the birthday in a few months as a date to aim for. I asked her not to feel pressured, to decide when the time was right for her, but at least she was warming to the idea. Here were the signs of something positive; of her desire to realise she was not alone in this scenario. In hindsight, we should have let her know sooner the effect her illness was having on all our lives and how she was not unique in her suffering, but we were never brave enough.

The other contributory factor in Shelley's recovery was Bella, a rescue Staffy–Alsatian cross, who was acquired at about the same time. She had been taken to the RSPCA in a terrible condition, starving to death, having kept her puppies alive. She had been in the kennels longer than was recommended and had no real takers, so she had been advertised for rehoming in a local paper.

Coincidentally, at this time Shelley and Neil had started their search for a dog, and it was love at first sight. Strangely, this thin, mentally scarred social outcast, who appeared aggressive to all who came near, warmed to Shelley, and she to her. I firmly believe dogs' power to sense and identify with human plights; did Bella sense Shelley's needs and vulnerability, and did Shelley see her own plight in canine form? Whatever it was, the attraction was great and a week later Bella had a new home. Shelley and Neil even got into the local paper for rehoming her, and later received a letter from a local man who had wanted to rescue Bella but was quite elderly. He thanked them, and they in turn wrote to him and sent him photographs.

From these events we have never looked back. The birthday meal was a great occasion, with Shelley eating three courses, in front of the family, for the first time in five-plus years. Then there was the weekend by the sea for Shelley, Emily and me, staying in a hotel and eating, although at this stage Shelley was often unwell after eating and it was very much two steps forward and one back. She persevered, however. I was amazed.

It is now that I have to eat a large slice of humble pie

and admit I was wrong to doubt Neil. Neil has stuck by Shelley; he has had the strength to stand up to her when needed and, through his unconditional love, has pulled her through. He said he 'would get there', and he has. He has had to live with Shelley, take her mood swings, suffer the hurt, live a lonely social existence, often without Shelley by his side, and be man enough to do it for the sake of his love for her. Neil, we commend you. You saw further than we did. You took the hurt and the torment but were in a position to do what we could not; you loved her directly and had a vision that she would be well. You were positive and believed that she would be well, even in the deepest depths of despair. You did what we could not, even though we tried so very hard.

Christmas 2006 was amazing. We met as an entire family for a Christmas meal at the hotel where Shelley and Neil had married. Shelley ate well and looked so happy, and so it has continued since. She has been studying for a degree at home, holding down a responsible job she enjoys, and has even acquired a piano and is teaching Neil to play. Bella continues to be their 'family'. Shelley and Neil's love for each other is obvious. They now holiday together, socialise together and at long last seem to be enjoying their lives as they should.

The knock-on effect for Emily is obvious too; she has her sister, her soulmate, back, and is looking forward to Shelley being bridesmaid at her wedding to Kev next year. All roses? I doubt it. Life isn't like that, but for now it is sunny again.

Why Shelley was ill, why she now is well, we will never

truly know. It was like a lightbulb being turned off and on. First it was sudden, unknown darkness, and now the light is back. Let us hope the bulb is a long-life one and the switch well out of reach!

If you read this out of curiosity, then I hope you have entered our thoughts and feelings and come away better informed. If you are a sufferer or a troubled carer, take solace in the hope that this illness can be beaten, no matter how hopeless things appear. My advice is to love the sufferer, unconditionally, helping them to rebuild their self-belief and turn their inward focus towards others. Encourage them to make the most of what they have, without fear of recrimination. Finally, hold them safe in your prayers until they are strong enough to reach out for their own salvation, and be prepared to champion their cause if they have sunk too far. You are not betraying them; you are saving them.

Perhaps most importantly, be prepared to do your worst! If I hadn't sectioned Shelley when I did, I'm certain she would not be alive today. She has actually thanked me for saving her life and said she would never have been able, in her diminished state, to accept that she needed to get professional help, or any help. As a parent the most selfless thing you can do is save your child, even at the cost of temporarily 'losing' them. You have to put self-interest on hold, summon up all your innermost strength and make them well. In my experience it will only make your love for each other stronger – but I warn you, you may have to wait!

Afterword

My story ended on a happy note with Shelley newly married, but much has happened since. She is now divorced and has a new, much younger boyfriend whom she seems very happy with. They enjoy lots of holidays and meals out, and that thrills me! She has also moved to an old cottage, one of her ambitions, and is gradually bringing it up to scratch.

She sadly lost her soulmate Bella the dog last year, aged over fifteen, but seems to be coping, although I know she misses her greatly.

She now has her university degree and is working in a job directly related to it.

I know the illness still lurks and sometimes, inadvertently, I say things that she takes as a criticism and is hurt by. She never tells me directly, but I find out from her sister and feel terrible as I forget that she is still very vulnerable.

However, the greatest news of all is that SHE IS ALIVE! She is eating, is a healthy weight and looks beautiful. Our loving daughter has returned from the dark place that was enslaving her and our relationship is intact, loving and oh-so-good! Yes, she has bad moments and challenges in her life (that is normal), but she seems to be coping well and no longer lets it control her.

Finally, my message to all sufferers of anorexia and to

anyone experiencing mental health problems is simply this: love yourself and your creation. Don't listen to media pressure, which at best presents an unattainable picture of perfection, even for Adonis himself, but celebrate your uniqueness. Love yourself and others, accepting their help and working with and not against their efforts. Face your demons and be determined that they will not rob you of your life and future.

Good luck; with help and prayer you *can* do it!
Thank you for listening.

Bonnie Forester
March 2019